Twayne's United States Authors Series

Sylvia E. Bowman, *Editor*

INDIANA UNIVERSITY

James Agee

TUSAS 252

Photograph courtesy of Helen Levitt

James Agee

James Agee

By VICTOR A. KRAMER

Georgia State University

TWAYNE PUBLISHERS

A DIVISION OF G. K. HALL & CO., BOSTON

Library of Congress Cataloging in Publication Data

Kramer, Victor A
  James Agee.

  (Twayne's United States authors series   ; TUSAS 252)
  Bibliography: p. 173-77.
  Includes Index.
  1.   Agee, James, 1909-1955—Criticism and interpre-
tation.
PS3501.G35Z74   818'.5'209   74-23882
ISBN 0-8057-0006-4

For my Parents
Leota and Edward Kramer

Contents

About the Author

Victor A. Kramer received the A. B. degree from Saint Edward's University in 1961, and the Ph.D. from the University of Texas at Austin in 1966. He has written extensively about James Agee, as well as about Horace Gregory, Sylvia Plath, Hart Crane, Robert Frost, and Frederick Law Olmsted. He teaches at Georgia State University and during 1974-1975 was Senior Fulbright Lecturer at the University of Regensburg in West Germany.

Preface

The writings of James Agee are diverse, but his poetic sensibility is fundamental to all he accomplished. Throughout his writing, from poetry to informal criticism, a consistency is revealed in his reverence for actuality. He was so concerned at times that actuality be honored that he argued for a blurring of distinctions between art and life. Agee saw and loved the world in its immediacy, and he was angered when others (with words, or improper use of camera) failed to see it. Correspondingly, his writing manifests an increasingly precise observation of the ordinary.

Agee's literary work constitutes the act of perception. In 1945 he noted: "integrity means wholeness as well as intactness; [and] in that sense perhaps the obligation is to . . . use one's consciousness as broadly and leisurely as if this were a time of peace (as indeed it is, or should be, in each individual mind and soul.)"[1] Earlier he stated that the "most indispensable obligation of the true artist, or of anyone [is] to try, under whatever confusion of pressures, to understand and illuminate and conduct oneself in accordance with the truth, in so far as one experiences it."[2] Agee told Helen Levitt approximately a year before his death "that poetry had been his true vocation, the thing he was born to do, but that it was too difficult." Robert Fitzgerald speculates that he meant "the difficulty for everyone—not only for himself—of making true poetry" in the forties and fifties; but Fitzgerald also insists "what he was born to do, he did."[3]

No point is gained in lamenting what he did not accomplish. His literary work possesses integrity. At times he relied upon satire or sarcasm, but even that posture reveals the truth as he experienced it. His unfinished manuscript for *A Death in the Family* is, above all, an affirmation of life. Those fictionalized memories demonstrate that Agee achieved the "inner vitality, and harmony, and integrity," which is the proper "business of the artist."[4]

This study documents Agee's conviction that poetry resides in the commonplace and depends upon remembrance. His film criticism, many projected ideas for analysis, and his prose also reveal this conviction. Just as the wide visions of Walt Whitman and William Carlos Williams allowed a broad poetic awareness, Agee's inclusiveness permitted him to see diverse materials and their relatedness. He produced many varieties of writing. Numerous drafts and revisions accompanied each project; large amounts of energy were expended even with film criticism or *Time* stories, and the care exercised in writing *Let Us Now Praise Famous Men* is an example of this precision. In that effort, the remembrance of the subject's texture remained relatively clear, but the writing seemed to make it confused. Writing about what had been experienced and projecting what was felt became an effort to recapture "the cruel radiance" of the *un*imagined.[5]

To be true to the experience as recalled and as modified by the imagination, *Famous Men* grew into a many-layered, personal reconstruction. Through no accident, much of Agee's writing is biographical. Even short stories written at Exeter or Harvard demonstrate that his fiction based on remembrance was apt to be clearer than that based on an artificially constructed plot. "Near the Tracks" seems a cliché in construction when compared with the more personal "Death in the Desert." Agee did not seek to obtain the distance of Henry James, for his forte was an ability to embody what revealed his feelings (or feelings of characters, often an extension of himself).

This study is concerned primarily with Agee's literary work; but his letters, criticism, and scripts also provide facets of information about a writer who wrote in many modes. John Huston has stated it was "all poetry," but Agee's screenplays are ultimately only instruments used in the making of films; therefore, minimal attention is given them. A fuller consideration of this part of his career is provided in Peter Ohlin's *Agee*. and Alfred Barson's *A Way of Seeing*. Instead, this book provides an analysis of all the significant published work of Agee as well as consideration of all available unpublished materials which are directly related to his accomplishment as a writer. The primary aim has been to explain the significant aspects of Agee's writing for readers who seek information about a particular work, or about the continuity of his career. Because Agee continued to develop throughout his career, his works are discussed chronologically. The first chapter provides an overview of his life as it relates to his career and developing aesthetic, but subsequent sections trace and analyze the growth of his literary production. Since *Let Us Now Praise Famous Men* and *A Death in the Family* are his major accomplishments, separate chapters are devoted to these works. A second goal of the book is to make available the results of extensive study of unpublished Agee material.

This study of James Agee was assisted by the generosity of many people; and, above all, three who know Agee well are the recipients of my gratitude. Mrs. Mia Agee, Reverend James Harold Flye, and Mr. David McDowell have each provided information and answered my questions on many occasions, either through correspondence or interviews. Their love for Agee has helped me to see the man and his writing more clearly. All readers of Agee are in debt to David McDowell's editorial work which made Agee's writing available.

I also thank the staff of the Humanities Research Center of The University of Texas at Austin where the James Agee papers are now housed, for each chapter in this study relies upon these materials. During my visits to that library from 1964 to the present, I can truly say it was always a pleasure to work with Mrs. Mary Hirth, Mr. John Payne, and other staff members. I am also indebted to many who have written about Agee. I wish especially to acknowledge my appreciation of the work of Alfred Barson, Jack Behar, Peter Ohlin, Sister Jeanne M. Concannon, John J. Snyder, Charles Mayo, and J. Douglas Perry, Jr. To my colleagues John Burrison, Thomas Scheer, and Alfred Barson, who read parts of this manuscript, I extend my thanks. Their suggestions have been a help. My thanks go also to Joseph Evans Slate and to Gordon Mills, who encouraged me during my initial study of Agee from 1963 to 1966. A large debt of gratitude also is acknowledged to the James Agee Trust, which has made unpublished Agee manuscript available for scholarly use. Dwight Macdonald also generously provided copies of Agee's correspondence to him.

The writing of this book was facilitated through time granted by the School of Arts and Sciences of Georgia State University during the winter quarter of 1972.

My main debt is to Dewey and Jerome.

VICTOR A. KRAMER

Georgia State University, Atlanta, Georgia.
University of Regensburg, Regensburg, Bavaria

Acknowledgments

The James Agee Trust has granted permission to quote from the Agee Papers at The University of Texas at Austin.

The uncollected poem "Rapid Transit" is used with the permission of the James Agee Trust.

From *The Collected Poems of James Agee*, Copyright 1968, Houghton Mifflin Co., permission has been granted to reprint (from *Permit Me Voyage*) "The Happy Hen," and "Sonnet XXV," "A Lover's Dialogue," and "Resolution." Calder and Boyars, Ltd., of London, has also granted permission to use these poems.

From *A Death in the Family* by James Agee. Copyright © 1957 by James Agee Trust. Reprinted by permission of the publisher, Grosset & Dunlap, Inc.

From *Agee on Film: Volume I* by James Agee. Copyright © 1957 by James Agee Trust. Reprinted by permission of the publisher, Grosset & Dunlap, Inc.

From *Agee on Film: Volume II* by James Agee, "The Bride Comes to Yellow Sky" by James Agee. Copyright © 1958 by Theasquare Production, Inc. Reprinted by permission of the publisher Grosset & Dunlap, Inc.

From *The Texas Quarterly* permission has been granted to reprint the first sonnet of "November 1945" from the group of "Three Sonnets."

From *The Mississippi Quarterly* permission has been granted to incorporate five paragraphs from my "Agee's *Let Us Now Praise Famous Men*: Image of Tenant Life."

I also want to express my thanks for Sylvia E. Bowman's editorial suggestions and for Elizabeth Holthaus's assistance in seeing this book through the press.

Chronology

1909   James Rufus Agee born November 27 in Knoxville, Tennessee.
1916   Death of his father, Hugh James Agee.
1919   Entered St. Andrew's, a boarding school near Sewanee, Tennessee.
1924- Attended Knoxville High School, Knoxville, Tennessee.
1925
1925   Entered Phillips Exeter Academy, Exeter, New Hampshire.
1928   Entered Harvard College.
1932   Graduated from Harvard; became a reporter for *Fortune*.
1933   Married to Olivia Saunders.
1934   Published *Permit Me Voyage*.
1935- Leave of absence from *Fortune*; lived and wrote in Anna
1936   Maria, Florida.
1936   Traveled through the South to gather material for study of tenant farmers.
1939   Divorced from Olivia Saunders; married to Alma Mailman; began reviewing for *Time*.
1941   Published *Let Us Now Praise Famous Men*.
1942   Began column on films in *The Nation*.
1944   Divorced from Alma Mailman; married to Mia Fritsch.
1948   Wrote commentary for Helen Levitt's film *The Quiet One*; film scripts based on Stephen Crane stories; began long autobiographical work.
1949   Published "Comedy's Greatest Era."
1950   Published "Undirectable Director."
1950- Wrote Screenplay for *The African Queen*.
1951
1951   Published *The Morning Watch*.
1952   Commissioned by Ford Foundation to do television script about Abraham Lincoln.
1952   Published "A Mother's Tale."

1953   Wrote screenplay for *Noa Noa.*

1954   Wrote screenplay for *The Night of the Hunter.*

1955   Died of heart attack in New York City, May 16.

CHAPTER 1

The Vocation of Writer

Art and actuality work on each other like live chemicals.
[Agee on Film]

I

J AMES Agee, while alive, was considered a genius with
words, and his diverse writings validate this appellation; but,
when commentators who knew him attempt to characterize his
writing, the result often is homage to a man whose personality was
luminous. His close friend, Irvine Upham, who first knew him while
both were aspiring writers at Harvard College, corroborates an
assertion made by Walker Evans that Agee's vocal prose "had
Elizabethan colors." Upham recalls that Agee's facility with
language was remarkable; and, like others, Upham insists that Agee
was even more gifted as a conversationalist than as a writer.[1] He
loved people and interchange with them; inevitably, this
characteristic is reflected in remembrances of him. Thus, while the
writing stands alone, the strength of Agee as a person remains fundamentally important; he did honor to living. Ultimately to ignore
Agee the man is impossible if one is to appreciate the writing. His
best prose grew directly from personal experience. A problem that
some critics would hasten to add is that Agee did not husband his
talents; he sought too much and too many kinds of accomplishment
which resulted in an overextension of talent and energy. Such a
generalization may contain truth; but, on the terms given and
accepted by him, his career was a happy one. He was a poet, a journalist, a novelist, a critic, and a scenarist; but, whenever he was asked what he did for a living, he significantly insisted with
characteristic simplicity that he was a "writer."[2] Agee arrested
many moments within a world which, for him, was always best
perceived in the full and continuous weight of its reality. Samuel

Taylor Coleridge, whom he admired, wrote that, if a poet properly apprehends any particular, it has the potential of suddenly taking on universality; and Agee, as writer, was continually concerned with rendering particularity through language so as to suggest universality.

II *The Tennessee Background*

Agee's family was in many ways ordinary, for it combined qualities of a rural background from his father's side with the more gently bred ancestry of his mother. His father, Hugh James Agee, the son of a mountain family from north of Knoxville, was born in 1880; and, while he worked in Panama for the postal service and in the city for several years, he retained many of the characteristics of his Tennessee ancestors, a family which can be traced back to the Virginia of 1688.[3] Agee's father has been described as having "a rugged sweetness, a tenderness, a fine chiseled handsomeness, a rollicking good humor, that made the heartbreak [of his unexpected death] irreparable."[4] James Agee's father died in an automobile accident when the son was six years old, and he was reared in the absence of his father. Years later, realization of the significance of that absence became a crucial fact for his artistic consciousness; he knew that his father had been a rugged individualist and that, had he lived, the son would have been formed differently.

Agee always remained aware of his Tennessee origins. He "never got far away from the simplicity of his Tennessee ancestors," and he "never lost the sound of the Tennessee mountain ballads that his father sang to him as a child."[5] Agee's mother commented that, as an aspiring writer, he was preoccupied with the loss of his father; and as early as age sixteen, he indicated that he wanted to write about the death and its effect upon the family. Nonetheless, Agee's early life was a happy one. The home in Knoxville was only two blocks from his mother's parents. Rufus, the name Agee was always called by his family, is remembered as being quick-witted and verbal—a precocious child, who at an early age "preferred stories of knights and dragons rather than the usual type of fairy tales." No doubt his mother, and perhaps also her family (a brother who lived in Knoxville was an artist) encouraged him in such matters. As a child he was often solitary, "a boy who had never learned to play baseball."[6]

Agee's mother, Laura Whitman Tyler, the daughter of a promi-
nent businessman, came from a "substantial family of artists and
musicians." And, in contrast to her husband, she represented for
Agee "all that was elegant and delicate and charming."[7] A graduate
of The University of Tennessee, she was interested in drama and
music, and she was a devout Episcopalian. For three years after her
husband's death, Mrs. Agee continued to live in the same neighborhood close to her family. During the summer of 1918 she visited
St. Andrew's School, located near Sewanee, Tennessee; and,
perhaps because of the religious atmosphere, she returned in 1919
to reside on the school grounds. Father James Harold Flye, who was
to become one of Agee's closest friends and who was then a teacher
at St. Andrews, explained her decision to stay on and enroll her
children there. The religious atmosphere appealed to her, and the
possibility of men teachers for Rufus seemed a good idea. Mrs. Agee
remained in residence adjacent to the school grounds for five years;
and in 1925 she married Father Erskine Wright who was on the
staff. Agee, in later life, realized that he had been heavily influenced by the religious attitudes of his mother; as a result, he devoted
considerable energy in the 1930s to extricating himself from the
hold of formal religion.

One of his classmates at St. Andrew's recalls that student life in
the school in the early 1920s was "rough, but good. Life was certainly not idyllic, . . . the student body was composed largely of
poor mountain boys, fifteen to twenty percent of whom were
orphans."[8] Agee's academic record was good, but apparently he
showed no literary interest during these years. Perhaps the most important thing which happened during the five years at St. Andrew's
was the friendship he developed with Father Flye. Robert
Phelps comments that "in almost no time, Rufus had become a
sort of foster son [for the Flyes]". Between Agee and Father Flye
"there developed the extraordinary quality of candor and
trust . . . reflected in the letters. . . ."[9] Those letters, which were
begun in 1925, continued to his death; and they attest to the
strength of their friendship.

By 1924, when only fourteen, Agee left St. Andrew's to attend
high school in Knoxville. That year allowed him to become familiar
with the Knoxville which he later captured in works of remembrance like *A Death in the Family*. That year also provided material

for some of his earliest literary production—the fiction, poetry, and drama published at Exeter.

In the summer of 1925 Agee and Father Flye made a trip to Europe, Agee's only visit to Europe. In the fall of that year he enrolled at Phillips Exeter Academy. At Exeter he participated in track and swimming, entered into musical activities, and joined a fraternity.[10] But most importantly his intense concern with writing and the problems which a writer faces emerged.

III   *Exeter and Harvard*

The atmosphere of Phillips Exeter was an intellectually stimulating one for Agee, who "found a great many interests he loved and many boys with similar tastes to his own."[11] Most importantly, he became editor of the *Phillips Exeter Monthly*; and his own contributions to the *Monthly* were so ambitious that one of his teachers described him as a "literary phenomenon." He wrote poetry, prose, drama, and reviews; and, while much is flawed as literature, this output demonstrates his multiplicity of interests. As early as 1927, when he wrote to Dwight Macdonald about the movies, he expressed his doubts about conventional literary forms: "every kind of recognized 'art' has been worked pretty nearly to the limit."[12] But such doubts did not prevent his enthusiastic production of poetry, plays, and fiction. Only one work, "Ann Garner," from this developmental period is known, as it was later slightly revised for *Permit Me Voyage*.

After Agee was graduated from Exeter, he went to Harvard; and the Agee of those years is most clearly revealed in Robert Fitzgerald's portrait "A Memoir": ". . . a rangy boy, alert and gentle, but sardonic, with something of the frontiersman or hillman about him—a hard guy in more than the fashion of the time—wearing always a man's clothes, a dark suit and vest, old and uncared for. . . . His manner . . . was undergraduate with discrimination."[13] At Harvard, Agee, who was able to prove himself as a writer, produced a good deal of prose and poetry; and he again served as an editor of a literary magazine, *The Harvard Advocate*. Much of his undergraduate writing, especially the prose, is now recognized as important in regard to his later accomplishments for his own experiences support this work. The summer of 1929 spent as a day laborer and harvest hand in Oklahoma, Kansas, and Nebraska was—like his experiences gleaned from knowledge of Knoxville, and from his bicycle tour of Europe—later used in his fiction. Although the years at Harvard assured the young Agee that he might become a good writer, much of his college writing seems derivative, although it is technically competent.

What is clear from the writing that he did before he was twenty-two is that, without the economic crisis of the early 1930s, Agee might have been able to support himself through fiction and poetry because of his ability and commitment. In letters of his college years he continually asserts his enthusiasm about a literary career: "I'm from now on committed to writing with a horrible definiteness." Nonetheless, he often seemed unsatisfied with merely conventional modes of writing—the fictional and poetic forms which he had mastered. By late 1931 he already sensed a need to write "as if . . . composing music." By 1932, he indicated that he felt "a great deal of poetry is the product of adolescence . . . and that as this state of mind changes, poetry is likely to dry up."[14] He meant that a poet necessarily must retain his adolescent enthusiasm if poetry were to be produced, and for him poetic enthusiasm was fading.

With his undergraduate years behind him, writing in conventional modes become increasingly more difficult. Nevertheless Harvard had provided a chance to prove he could write, and a freedom and leisure to live without economic pressure, something he never again experienced. In 1932, when he sought a job after graduation, he, like many others, had little choice but to accept the first position offered him. He obtained a job with *Fortune* magazine, which was ironic since he had, while editor of the *Advocate*, coordinated an elaborate parody of *Time* magazine.

IV   *The Promise of the 1930s*

Agee's educational experiences were beneficial. The intimacy of St. Andrew's and the friendship of Father Flye were valued throughout life. The chance to attend an excellent preparatory school had helped him to develop his talent; and the years at Harvard were later recalled by him as "the best years of his life." But, since he hoped to continue his education, he applied for a fellowship to Oxford or Cambridge but with no results. The position with *Fortune* magazine must have been taken with a hope that it would leave some time for creative work; and he not only wrote poetry during his early New York years but also began to collect short stories for a book which never materialized. In 1934, a volume of his poems was published as part of the Yale Series of Younger Poets. But his position as staff writer for a business publication was hardly the work for which he had been preparing, and finally the role of journalist became a source of frustration. His commitment to writing seemed to be leading nowhere. Since he felt that his own writing was the most important thing, he was beginning to feel desperate by 1933. He wrote Father Flye: ". . . little writing as I've done, and little confidence as I've a right to, I still feel that life is short and that no earthly thing is as important to me as learning how to write. And for that you *must* have time!"[15]

He was surely constricted by writing assigned pieces on set topics to be published anonymously. His prose for *Fortune* was rather carefully edited so that the literary style of an aspiring young artist would not detract from the ultimately utilitarian nature of the magazine; but his characteristics were not wholly eliminated. Some of those *Fortune* pieces do have an unmistakable Agee rhetorical quality.

Certainly Agee saw the advantage of having a job, but already during his first months in New York he apparently hoped for a way to escape. He wrote: "I care very little about my job, except for my own writing and whatever may help me in it."[16] Given his ability and sensitivity he was not long in New York before what he described as an "epidemic of despair and weariness" began to overtake him. And while he could write enthusiastically about listening to Beethoven's Ninth Symphony in an empty skyscraper late at night, the "spiritual *tone* of [the] time" seemed to him "the darkest and saddest in centuries."[17]

Later he began to raise objections about his education. He wondered, somewhat romantically, if perhaps a library and the chance for friendship might not have been as effective a means of education. Several more years after Harvard (when writing *Famous Men*), he expressed doubts about his education; but to do so was a fundamental part of Agee's nature. He was seldom interested in accepting things without question, and he loved to take a subject and argue it at length. Almost as much pleasure could be obtained in arguing an opposed position.[18]

Early in 1933 he married Olivia Saunders; however, that

marriage lasted only five years. He planned many different writing projects during those years, but only a few poems were published. For the most part, he felt he was unable to channel his artistic energy as he needed to do.[19] He continued as journalist, in large part because other jobs were not available; and, just as ironically as his having obtained his first job, through a parody of *Time* magazine, the chance to write *Let Us Now Praise Famous Men* was the result of an initial assignment by *Fortune*. Letters to Father Flye and recollections of Robert Fitzgerald indicate that Agee was quite enthusiastic about the project for he had theorized for years about how new nonfiction writing could be developed. When he learned in the spring of 1936 that he and Walker Evans would be sent to Alabama, he was exuberant. His subsequent expansion of the tenant material into a book after *Fortune* refused publication may have caused him finally to break with *Fortune*. He contributed only a few articles in 1936 and 1937, and by 1938 he was at work rewriting and restructuring parts of *Let Us Now Praise Famous Men*.

In 1937 he applied, in a second unsuccessful attempt, for a Guggenheim Fellowship. His interests were many and his hopes remained high during these years. In his 1960 essay, Walker Evans remembers Agee's complexity in this way: "I think he felt he was elaborately washed, but what you saw right away—alas for con-spiracy—was a faint rubbing of Harvard and Exeter, a hint of fami-ly gentility, and a trace of romantic idealism. . . . He didn't look much like a poet, an intellectual, an artist, or a Christian, each of which he was. Nor was there outward sign of his paralyzing, self-lacerating anger." Agee's interests derive from all these qualities, but he usually planned more than he could accomplish.

Evans recalls that "physically Agee was quite powerful, in the deceptive way of uninsistent large men. His hands were large, long, bony, light, and uncared for. His gestures were one of the memorable things about him."[20] Others have commented on his ability to mimic and provide gestures appropriate to his many moods. His ambitious plans for work in 1937 (submitted with the Guggenheim application) are still another indication of his energetic interests. The "Plans" run to several pages and almost fif-ty separate projects are listed. These range from the conventional to the totally unexplored. Analysis; nonfiction; revues; films;

letters—all were possibilities. Although the Guggenheim judges must have been baffled by what Agee suggested he might do, his unorthodox listing of projects demonstrates how he was gradually moving away from conventional categories of writing.

While Agee's hopes for writing multiplied during the late 1930s, his personal life became more difficult. In addition to financial problems, the first marriage ended in divorce in 1939; and during that same year he married Alma Mailman. In 1940, his first son, Joel, was born. But the second marriage did not last either, and one of his unpublished manuscripts for a short story seems to suggest the turmoil of this period. The story is partly autobiographical, and some of the mood which informed Agee's New York experience is suggested from the story, probably written about 1939.[21] Its setting is a party at a Greenwich Village apartment, and the tone is established through the blasé attitude that its characters have about a divorce which two are planning. Two characters, Alice and Harvey, get into a loud argument and a screaming session because during the party, apparently, Alice had been caught by Harvey, her husband, in a compromising situation in the bedroom.

V   *The Frustration and Discipline of the 1940s*

While still writing *Famous Men*, Agee began reviewing books for *Time* magazine in late 1939, but he later shifted to reviewing films, and he continued to write such reviews through 1948. Beginning in 1941 he also began to write a regular film column for *The Nation*, and through that bi-weekly column his reputation as an authority on the cinema developed. Although his film criticism eventually provided an entry into the writing of screenplays, Agee undoubtedly wondered if he would ever find sufficient time for "his own writing." He realized that he lacked, and severely needed, discipline. Yet ironically, precisely because he was interested in so many different kinds of things, he was able to accomplish what he did. He knew that to put everything he had into each opportunity was finally a waste. The tales, now almost legend, about how he devoted an inordinate amount of energy to rewriting a story for *Time* magazine, or took months on a task others would have done more quickly, are numerous. He would stay up all night to talk with someone if he felt there was the slightest need.

Agee knew he made mistakes and he was able to castigate himself for lack of discipline: "Mr. Agee has interested himself in writing only during the past seventeen years. . . . He has done little of his own 'stuff' during the past two years, being far too fascinated by what he laughingly calls his 'private' 'life,' and by his task of book-reviewing for one of the great weekly magazines. 'Why write,' he queries, 'when one may read, and read, and read, the superb work which is done by others?' "[22] This sarcastic commentary was composed by him in 1943, at perhaps one of the lowest psychological points in his career. *Let Us Now Praise Famous Men* did not sell well; and he was doing practically none of "his own writing."

While Agee's film criticism was appreciated by many readers, its method, essentially subjective, was in effect Agee talking as an "amateur" about the complexity of something he enjoyed; for he never regarded a film in simplistic terms. In his criticism he put himself into the position of viewer, and he saw a film as a combination of problems, attitudes, points of view, and materials available, all of which brought about a particular object. Being able to put himself into the frame of mind of another was his fundamental characteristic as critic and person. When David McDowell remarked that Agee was the closest to a saint of any person he had ever known, he penetrated the core of Agee's personality; for at its center was a selflessness which allowed him to feel what others felt as well.[23]

An irony of Agee's life was that, despite his sure ability to feel with others, his personal life remained tortured. He was married three times, and only with his third marriage, to Mia Fritsch, did his life begin to attain the degree of order necessary for writing. This final marriage, which brought three more children, provided a domestic stability which he had not before experienced. Also, in 1946 he purchased a small farm outside the city at Hillsdale, New York; and there he loved doing his writing. By the late 1940s, he had established a life-rhythm which promised to allow time for fiction.

By late in the decade he terminated his regular work for *Time* and began to do free-lance scriptwriting. Several screenplays resulted from this period; and, while he himself described this writing as "hack work," his scenario writing was accompanied by the promise of free time. Unfortunately, Agee seems to have come only very slowly to the conclusion that contracted scenario writing

was in many ways akin to the earlier journalistic writing for *Fortune*
or *Time*. Although he regarded the screen work as a temporary job
which would provide leisure, his success as a screenplay writer led
to other commitments; but during the months before his death he
did talk seriously about taking the summer to finish *A Death in the
Family*, the autobiographical novel he had begun in 1948.

After 1948 the bulk of his energy was devoted to scriptwriting;
and, while some of his work was never produced, a good amount
was because he was clearly a capable filmwriter. During this period
he wrote screenplays for over a dozen films; and, from some points
of view, the loss of poetry or fiction which Agee might have produced is tragic. In January, 1951, while working in Hollywood with
John Huston on the screenplay for *The African Queen*, Agee suffered the first of a series of heart attacks, the initial signal that he
was in bad health. Only a few years later he died on May 16, 1955,
from a heart attack while riding in a taxicab in New York City.

VI *A Developing Aesthetic*

Agee doubtless was incapable of taking a news story or a script
and doing it with his left hand as others might have, because he was
too conscientious. Perhaps he was taken advantage of as he earned
his living; but, as the meditation "Work" in *Famous Men* makes
clear, all work is a cheated ruin—the thing through which anyone
stays alive but that which also destroys the worker. William
Faulkner's screen writing supported him; Agee's liability of
lavishing attention on details simply consumed all of his energy. But
this method is both a deficiency and the value of what he was and
did.

In whatever Agee wrote he sought an appropriate mode of
transfiguring the texture of commonplace experience. He was
fascinated with the daily events of living which were intertwined
with death; and, although he respected life above art, he accepted
the challenge given any poet. He once wrote, "words cannot embody; they can only describe"; but the poet realizes this basic
deficiency and accepting it "continually brings words as near as he
can to an illusion of embodiment."[24] Agee also insisted "that
creative imagination is the only possible substitute for the plainest
sort of good sense—and is, after all, merely an intensification of
good sense to the point of incandescence."[25] The poet is able to dis-

till the ordinary in an extraordinary way and to present his knowledge through language; he is able to reorder reality. Often, as one reads Agee's works, he is reminded of Agee's fascination with the beauty of minute intersections of time, space, and consciousness. One of his earliest stories, "They That Sow in Sorrow Shall Reap" (1931), interestingly, contains a section of literary criticism much like the central part of "On The Porch" in *Famous Men*; and in this story he indicates his concern, his problem, and his despair with finding the means to record ordinary details of consciousness. He complained:

I fail to carry one idea through; before I realize it, I am whirled along the rim of another—and so on—ad nauseam.
Yet, from time to time, I am aware of a definite form and rhythm and melody of existence. . . . And at that moment—or rather, through its reverberations in our brain, the whole commonplaceness of existence is transfigured—becomes monstrously powerful, and beautiful, and significant—assuming these qualities validly but unanswerably—, and descends through tangled discords, once more into commonplaceness, with nothing answered, nothing gained, and heaven undisturbed.[26]

In Chekhov's *The Cherry Orchard* such "melody was caught, and . . . great drama had been made. . ."; but Agee did not know how it had been achieved. As a young writer wishing his career he sensed that he would have to find language to transfigure the commonplace. He knew that an accurate means of reflecting the world necessitated a structure: "I'd do anything on earth to become a really good writer. . . . Do you see, though, where it leads me? . . . I have no faith to speak of in my native ability. . . . My intellectual pelvic girdle is simply not Miltonically wide."[27] Such self-doubt, combined with distractions of doing writing he really did not enjoy, sometimes made it difficult to write. But the magnitude of his hopes provided a sufficient momentum, and part of what he desired to accomplish is reflected in another portion of the letter in which he suggests he might combine the "eventless beauty" of Chekhov with the "huge geometric plots" of Shakespeare: ". . . to do the whole so that it flows naturally, and yet, so that the whole—words, emotions, characters, situation, etc.—has a discernible symmetry and a very definite *musical* quality—inaccurately speaking—I want to *write symphonies*. That is, characters introduced quietly (as are themes in a symphony, say) will recur in new lights, with new verbal orchestration, will work into counterpoint and get a sort of monstrous grinding beauty—and so on."

Although Agee never wrote such "symphonies," part of his work does possess the themes and counterpoint about which he dreamed. In *A Death in the Family*, Rufus constantly encounters a world which is mysterious to him. The episodes from the child's point of view are woven together by the recurrence of motifs which emphasize loneliness or reconciliation, and these episodes in juxtaposition reverberate into something more than just themselves. The same effect is found in *Famous Men*, and a comparable method is apparent in the film criticism in which Agee's subjective approach results in commentary that moves beyond the immediacy of a particular film's analysis.

Agee's uses of language are often compared to the camera; however, the more clearly and intensely he perceives and is able to transfer that perception, the less he is like a mechanical producer of images. The artist's response is outward turning, and he grasps the world through an intricate texture of feeling. True, Agee realized a camera could capture an instant of time, and a photograph properly seen reveals immense amounts of knowledge; but he also knew that, to give the texture of feeling within a particular period of time, words possessed potentialities absent in photography precisely because a person is not a strip of film. Sometimes his preciseness of language suggests that he is attempting to write as a camera might reproduce reality, but his vision remains intensely humane, and his involvement contributes a lyrical quality.

Agee's love for the world was usually apprehended, as has been observed, through his careful observation of particulars. His early uncollected poem, "Rapid Transit," published in 1937, demonstrates how his clear apprehension of an event could lead to an expansion of concern toward its wider significance. Subway trains carry millions in a big city, and the blank faces of passengers reminded Agee of changes which a technological civilization brings:

> Squealing under city stone
> The millions on the millions run,

> Every one a life alone,
>> Every one a soul undone:
>
> There all the poisons of the heart
>> Branch and abound like whirling brooks,
> And there through every useless art
>> Like spoiled meats on a butcher's hooks
>
> Pour forth upon their frightful kind
>> The faces of each ruined child:
> The wrecked demeanors of the mind
>> That now is tamed, and once was wild.[28]

"Rapid Transit" is startling; but its clarity derives from its rather conventional images ("whirling brooks" and "city stone"), which do not emphasize an immediacy of apprehension. In the harshness of image and stark vision of the city the influence of Blake is apparent. Most of Agee's later poetry is not written in such traditional poetic molds, but it is both more limited in perspective and precise in observation.

Although Agee's career began with the mastery of traditional verse forms, his career is best described as a development of means whereby the texture of events could be embodied for their own sake. As he matured artistically, he realized that he did not need to be burdened with the implications of what was perceived; instead, he limited himself to what was observed. The achievement of aesthetic distance, to maintain a balance between particular things observed and universals which were associated with them, became possible. His ability to write while maintaining distance is bound up with his realization of the inherent beauty of the quotidian. Tiny facets of actuality, carefully beheld and written about, become the objects of Agee's attention.

Agee was, as Walker Evans has remarked, "a born sovereign prince of the English Language." But Agee was also a special kind of person. Open and interested, quickwitted and aware of the complexity of all things in a complex universe, he was always beginning again, always looking again to see if there might be a different, or better, way of seeing and writing. His openness and complexity of thought led him to many tasks.

CHAPTER 2

The Early Production

I Phillips Exeter Beginnings

FATHER Flye recalls that during his and Agee's European tour of 1925, the sixteen-year-old Agee was regularly taking notes;[1] and some of those notes were soon transposed into literature. Phillips Exeter Academy provided an agreeable atmosphere for Agee as an aspiring artist; and his hopes of writing while there are well documented. His initial writing reflects enthusiasm, and one early piece even foreshadows his later interest in film. A 1926 essay "The Moving Picture" discusses Charlie Chaplin's genius, the technique of film making, the cameraman, and the significance of the director.[2] Most of Agee's earliest writing is derivative; but the variety of fiction, satire, and drama, which appeared in the *Phillips Exeter Monthly* from November, 1925, to June, 1928, demonstrates his propensity for what later became both a virtue and hindrance—his stubborn insistence on nonspecialization.

Other characteristics basic to his later literary works are also present in his writing while at Exeter. Agee's awareness of the transitoriness of human life and of man's fragility, a theme which later buttresses the poetry of *Permit Me Voyage*, is especially evident. In his early prose, Agee shaped his sense of the fraility of man's existence. In the sketches, "The Bell Tower of Amiens" and "The Scar," Agee delineates a young narrator's surprise when confronted with the devastation of war.[3] In both, Agee, who apparently developed material gathered during his visit to Europe, focuses on destruction and loss.

Other stories are set in Tennessee and have a humorous tone. "Knoxton High," obviously based upon memories of the year spent in Knoxville in 1924–25, satirizes small-town provincialism.[4] The story is Agee's first attempt at stream-of-consciousness, and it pokes fun at the pride taken in a new school building. Other Tennessee stories are more somber; for example, "The Circle" is a narrative of a young man trapped by his father's death.[5] The hero is destined to entrapment mostly because of his own laziness and his choice of a dull life in a small town. Another story which incorporates memories of Tennessee is "Minerva Farmer,"[6] in which Agee's knowledge of the University of Tennessee, as well as his memories of the grammar school where he had been a student, support a narrative about a woman who finally graduates from the university at age thirty-nine. She teaches for twenty years, but she is abruptly dismissed because of her harshness. While awkward, the story documents an early interest in recovering the past: Agee included the name of the principal he remembered from childhood. Sketchy in places, "Minerva Farmer" evokes the futility of much human effort.

"A Sentimental Journey," which has a related theme,[7] is about a young widow whose marriage had been considered undesirable by her family; and Agee again utilizes the stream-of-consciousness technique to build toward her choice of uncertainty, as opposed to the security of going back to family. Another of the early stories provides an account of a Negro funeral, and of it Concannon incorrectly states that "Bound for the Promised Land" is, "in kernel, the funeral chapter of the later *A Death in the Family*. . . . The satiric treatment of the clergyman and descriptions of both mourners and the deceased are used almost exactly thirty years later. . . ."[8] Although this statement is untrue, it correctly indicates the method by which Agee was beginning to fictionalize experienced materials—something fundamental for his later fiction.

An equally important source for creativity at Exeter was a knowledge of the classics. Agee produced three classical satires, and each is clever but limited. In the amusing "Phogias and Meion," the humor of victory and then defeat of a Greek hero who competes in the games is caused by a lack of knowledge about the city.[9] "Chivalry, an Allegory" is about heroism and knighthood,[10] and this satire undercuts the ideals of knighthood with the use of modern dialogue. "Sacre du Printemps" concerns the pursuit of Pan by a twentieth-century Miss Marcia Puff, and the incorporation of contemporary speech focuses the story. Each of these satires combines a knowledge of the classics and an interest in satiric humor.

Agee's experiments with drama at Exeter, like his prose, often rely upon his knowledge of classical literature; and he also attempted utilization of his Tennessee background. *In Vindication*, published in March, 1926, takes place in the home of Socrates.[12] Agee sets the satire in the kitchen of Xanthippe to demonstrate Socrates' complete failure to satisfy his wife; and the tone is, predictably, mocking. In the play *Catched*, which takes place in the interior of a log cabin in the Appalachian mountains,[13] the plot is predictable. Mag, the daughter of the Felts family, loses her virginity to a "city feller," Sam Hayden, who has no intention of marrying her; but her mountaineer lover, Ed Winters, does accept her. Agee's inclusion of mountain dialogue is skillfully executed. Another play, *Any Seventh Son*, also set in the mountains,[14] has as its theme the curse of a seventh son born to a seventh son: the drunken Jed kills his son when the midwife describes the deformed baby.

The most important of Agee's four Exeter dramas, *Menalcas*, is a one-act play modeled on early Greek drama;[15] but thematically, the plot is related to the mountain play *Any Seventh Son*. In this classical adaptation, Menalcas, the hero, is the only male survivor of Aeschinas. He has a daughter by whom he begets a son. That son is born an idiot: "malformed spawn" with "brain bereft." The chorus, the gods, and nature urge Menalcas to sacrifice the child; and he does so. Agee's sparse imitative language is successful. The chorus approaches the quantitative quality of classical verse, and a tragic tone is sustained. The pattern of images with "its shift from peace and life to war and death is strong and consistent throughout the poem."[17]

Agee reported to Father Flye that *Menalcas* received favorable criticism. S. Foster Damon had read it, and thought it good. Agee noted Damon gave him "some fifteen names and addresses to whom to send it for further criticism—Robert Frost, Edna St. Vincent Millay, Sara Teasdale, Robert Hillyer, Hilda Doolittle, Ezra Pound, etc."[16] In the same letter he continued enthusiastically: "I saw R. Frost this spring; showed him *Pygmalion* and *Menalcas*—He said even better things of it than S. Foster—later another man, James Rorty, had a shot at *Menalcas*, and thought it good.—The general verdict is that I can do a lot if I don't give up and write advertisements."

Agee's early lyrics tend to be abstract, but some of his earliest poetry seems to be an attempt to objectify the loss which Agee realized that he and family had sustained in the death of his father. These poems are also indicators of thematic interests, and "Ebb Tide" is a good example. Its speaker is aware that he is left alone, but he also recognizes that the cyclical nature of all things makes his separation only temporary. One is reminded of the fictionalized Rufus: "He's gone, he's dead. . . . My life—it's like a little shallow pool/ Left in a hollowed rock by ebbing tide." In the poetic monologue "Widow," the general emotion of "Ebb Tide" is more specific, for the single natural image of the sea in the former is focused upon one particular emotion. In this monologue, which appeared one year after "Ebb Tide,"[18] a widow trims her Christmas tree while she thinks of the "coffin lowered in the sifting snow/ Only this afternoon." Even though some rhymes are forced, the poem catches the conversational idiom.

The most mature poem Agee produced while at Exeter is "Anne Garner," the only poem from this earliest period which Agee later chose to republish.[19] Since his revised version appears in *Permit Me Voyage*, it is discussed in that context. "Anne Garner" combines Agee's thematic interests—a preoccupation with death and an interest in Tennessee regional material in that the Greek Pasiphaë myth is presented in an Appalachian mountain setting. Above all, the poem demonstrates a growing technical power.

Still another significant poem grew out of the Exeter years, the still unpublished "Pygmalion."[20] Whether or not the extant manuscript is the early "Pygmalion" Agee mentions in his 1928 correspondence remains uncertain. He never published a poem of this title; and the manuscript copy employs a later form of his name, "James" rather than the usual Exeter "J.R." or "James Rufus." Even if the manuscript poem is a later version of the 1928 "Pygmalion," the piece suggests what Agee was learning as an artist; it represents a transition from his earliest to more mature phase; and it is a correlative to his later artistic dilemma of finding a form adequate for his vision.[21] Parts of "Pygmalion" are similar to the abstract methods idiosyncratic to the earliest writing. Some sections are beautifully composed; other parts remain incomplete; and the abrupt ending seems to indicate that Agee had not finished forming an idea.

"Pygmalion" is a soliloquy spoken by the Creator who describes

His inception, formation, and destruction of the world: "a glorious dream," a statement that may be symbolic of the poet's creation. The poetic God is anthropomorphic; under His "subtle smoothing of . . . hands," the world was "molded out a warm rotundity." Effective imagery is found in the descriptions of seasons and of the physical characteristics of earth. In the fall of the year, the Creator enjoys beholding the leaves. It is a pleasure for Him

> . . . to hear
> One raucous groan of color, dying out
> As swirling leaf o'erlaps each fading leaf
> And drains [its] life-blood back into [its] breast. . . .[22]

Agee the lyric poet sees the change in the seasons, and with spurts of poetic language imbues the poem with life. The Creator's fondness for his world and his enjoyment in watching a particular "Spring, crouching noiselessly upon the hills" is clearly suggested; the ideas which support the poem however are not clear, and the poem is diffuse.

One would assume that God's "glorious dream" and the result of His creation would have been forever present in His mind. Yet at this poem's end the speaker's surprise seems as great as the reader's when he holds the "bruised and broken form of earth." In the poet's imagination the world is so beautiful that the Creator says he must "strain" it "close" in order ". . . to alleviate the agony/ Of such a passion as I never knew." Such a magnificent caress results in a world "bruised and broken." Possibly the shock of such an abrupt ending is what Agee intended; but, as a picture of the world's change, or as an evocation of God's love, the poem fails.

"Pygmalion" remains important, however, because Agee hints at his doubts about the myth of creation as accepted by traditional religion and because of suggestions about the difficulty of a poet's being satisfied with his artistic act. Only a few years later Agee found it increasingly difficult to rely upon a traditional framework of Christian thought upon which to build poetry. He was often concerned about ways to perfect his artistic talents, and this poem reflects the difficulty any artist experiences in shaping material into a satisfactory form. "Pygmalion" is, therefore, the earliest sustained poetic expression of Agee's realization of the problems of seeking appropriate means to embody his vision.

II *Harvard Refinements*

When Agee went to Harvard, he was already "committed to writing"; and his years there allowed him to prove that he could write and to produce a substantial amount of work. As a literature major, his concentration was in the Renaissance, and his undergraduate poems are often imitations of Elizabethan or Metaphysical works. Only eight Harvard poems were later included in *Permit Me Voyage*, seven of these being revisions for a sonnet sequence. The undergraduate writing, however, reflects a significant change in Agee's development. In the twenty-six poems published in *The Harvard Advocate* and in his class ode, one finds the manner in which he assimilated traditional writers.

The *carpe diem* theme is predominant, perhaps the most important single theme in this group of poems. "Apotheosis," an admonition for lovers that was written relatively early during these years, consists of only eight lines; but it is representative of Agee's accomplishment. Its speaker warns lovers to "make your kisses light," and to keep passions under control because only too soon the flesh slips away: "Down from the dull/ Dead bones, and lovers' lips/ Kiss but a skull." The theme of the transitoriness of the flesh is also basic to "The Shadow," "A Lover's Dialogue," "The Rendezvous," and "The Truce," as well as to the sonnets later incorporated in *Permit Me Voyage*.[23] A mature example of Agee's skill in treating the *carpe diem* theme is the "Sonnet," which appeared in a 1930 issue of the *Advocate*, in which the poet dwells on the paradoxical notion that living is a movement toward death. While man is unaware, death slowly comes and unexpectedly appears. The speaker realizes that "Even now, a serpent swells my living skull: / Its thirsty tongue, stands barbed through my brain. . . ."[24] Like "A Lover's Dialogue" and like "The Rendezvous," which both appeared in the early months of 1930, "Sonnet" reflects derivative characteristics.

Often either an Elizabethan or Metaphysical style flavors the diction, rhythm, and metaphor of the Harvard poems. Agee's adoption of traditional forms and archaic language reflects attempts to find a mode for expressing Christian beliefs; but this method never fully coalesced with his temperament. Because these poems are imitative in technique, their form imposes a barrier between perception and

projection of knowledge. Although these poems should be considered as exercises, they demonstrate a facile use of language and
control; but the conception of man's relation to the universe derives
from Agee's admiration of the Metaphysical poets. In "A Lover's
Dialogue," for instance, a single image is skillfully molded through
the length of the poem where both the *carpe diem* motif and the
Christian hope of resurrection are woven together: both are fused in
the symbol of a candle, and sensual and spiritual implications are
melded. Not to enjoy the body which has been provided by God
must, in one sense, prevent man from ever attaining fullness within
the spiritual life. The speaker says:

> "O, let me set to this new wick,
> Dry, and athirst for light, love's name.
> So, we may watch the slow descent
> Of wax ascend in steady flame.
>
> For thus, virginity grows small;
> Thus fails the firm and gallant flesh:
> But, surely as it burns to naught
> The soul arises, hot and fresh."
>
> "No, I shall keep the wick unsinged:
> The taper, white and whole and cool,
> Shall never dwindle uselessly.
> I shall preserve all."
>
> "Ah, sad fool,
> You think a selfish beauty lasts;
> Or, to bestow it whole were shame.
> Hear: A sure death encases it
> In one bright tube of instant flame!"[25]

Part of the success of the piece is the completely regular meter.
Even the half line of the third stanza merely pretends to break the
rigid structure, for the first part of the fourth stanza immediately
completes the expected pattern. The diction of the poem is conventional; "naught" seems purposely chosen for poetic flavor.

A step farther in the progress of the spiritual life is advocated in
"The Rendezvous," again based on the Christian dogma of the

resurrection. Man's "cloudy love" burns "to clearest air . . . before
the blazing God"; and thus in the last stanza the speaker ad-
monishes his lover:

> "Be sad no more;   forget me
>   As now I can you: lose in God your soul:
> Me, love's thin fever
>   Could not beguile from death's white ruinous coal!"[26]

Death is the single most important theme throughout these poems.
The abstract idea of it is to be recognized, accepted, and then incorporated poetically. In "Resolution" death is more concept than
reality:

> This fire that lances me about,
> This thunderous benumbing doubt,
> This ocean-rooted sheer of rain
> That brims the dark with smothering pain—
>
> This wrack of murderous storm shall melt
> Clean from the sky, and on the sky
> The long arrangèd stars have spelt
> A fate no storm can set awry.[27]

Such abstractions about death are a significant feature of this early
poetry, and Agee's technical excellence evinced in lines such as
these in "The Truce" is obvious:

> Time shall ravel us asunder:
> Mind's delight and body's wonder
> And our shrewd-contrivèd lust
> Time shall wither into dust.[28]

The colon in conjunction with the run-on lines to the end of the
passage reinforces the sense of the rhymes. "Shrewd-contrivèd"
suggests man's devious, intricate ways of justification which ultimately come to nothing; and the immediate juxtaposition of
"shrewd-contrivèd" with "lust" suggests the ugliness of man's
designs. The compactness of the second line and the use of "ravel"
to evoke the intricacy of man's action are precise. But the poem

remains heavily an abstraction; and the pity and inadequacy of human love is hardly suggested as a reality. Certainly this pity and the reality of death is not so clearly suggested in this poem as in the later one "Sunday: Outskirts of Knoxville, Tenn." In "Sunday," the imagery and rhythm grow from the poet's vision of the sadness of human love, and this poem appears to have developed from a precise observation of particular events and persons.

As an undergraduate, Agee already realized that any moment, unique in its particularity, could arrest man in a way that considerable intellectualizing would not. In "The Truce," his speaker knows that one can complain and criticize life and the inadequacy of love, but such criticism is irrelevant when particular moments in consciousness are intensely felt. However, Agee implies in the poem his awareness of the tremendous difficulty in arresting individual moments. Within this poem, Agee wrote:

> So much can our love attain,
> Just so much, and that with pain;
> Though we die to change the score
> Just so much, and nothing more.
> Pity need not be the passion
> Though it be our private fashion:
> Any single joy or grief
> Turns the trick that cracks belief;
> And the body's left behind
> Whispering to the abandoned mind [.]29

As a poet, Agee caught many single joys and griefs; but additional experimentation preceded those successes; and he apparently sensed the difficulty of what he must do as a writer. In a Christmas poem, written during his senior year, he asserts hopes for poetic accomplishment, but he expresses fear that he will not be able to find the key to such success. His poem begins with the realization that "all things of life" can be termed "as many doors." For some, doors swing wide with ease; for others, the uninitiated, mysteries must be sought: "Such a man am I" laments the speaker. Doors open for those who do not question or implore; those who ask too many questions cause hinges to spring; they find nothing, and only death awaits them. Despair results when one tries too hard to open truth, or force love; and finally there is but one door:

> . . . death: and through my chief assault
> And shrewdest labor I've assembled there,
> Dark hinges no conjecture may default
> Soon shall devolve me on a doorless air. [30]

This poem expresses a continued awareness of the need to write well, and a need to seek appropriate means. In brief, this poem is about vocation, but most especially about the poet's.

In contrast to the abstractness of the undergraduate poetry, Agee's early fiction often reflects his appreciation of the world of experience. Indeed, Fitzgerald states that the Harvard poetry never seemed to him to possess the rhythm and power of the prose. [31] Agee's best stories possess an immediacy which suggests he incorporated biographical material, for those stories that treat ideas are less successful. For instance, in one story a young father, horrified at what he feels and haunted by a sense of mortal sin, kills an unwanted child by hurling the infant over a cliff. In this concocted situation, somewhat ironically entitled "A Walk Before Mass," the weight of Christianity and the teachings of the church are a burden to the protagonist.[32] The story is no more successful than the Exeter drama *Any Seventh Son*, which it strongly resembles. While the narrative is about envy and maturity, motivation and characterization are not clear; and the only fact that is apparent is that the teachings of the church haunt the protagonist, and the child may be intended as symbol for the church. The story remains amorphous, perhaps because it is based too much on imagination; but other stories by Agee seem more believable because they concentrate upon perceptions of real things.

As has been indicated, one can separate the early prose into two groups; stories that seem to rely heavily upon imagination; and those which grew out of personal experience, or at least are limited to emotional experiences that someone as young as Agee could have experienced and adequately presented. "Boys Will Be Brutes" is successful because its apparent basis is in an actual, or a believably portrayed, experience. This story relates the slaughter of tiny birds after they had been taken from their nest. Generally, as an emotional and moral situation became more complex (or was perceived so), more skill was demanded of Agee to recreate that experience. As a result, Agee's early stories which deal with illicit love among the terribly poor, religion, alcohol, or an unfortunate pregnancy usually do not seem finished.

In contrast, stories written at about the same time which are more limited in scope are careful accomplishments. One of the best examples is "Death in the Desert," a story which limits itself in large part to the stream-of-consciousness revelation of the mind of the narrator. The narrator is a young man who appears to be much like the young Agee of age twenty; and his story, which is compellingly presented, relates the experience of a summer hitchhiker who has gotten a ride with a rather dull couple from Oklahoma across a desert of a hundred miles. While sitting in the back of their six-year-old Buick, he enjoys reflecting about the couple—even going so far as to mentally strip them of their clothes and to allow two grotesque skeletons to guide the Buick. Part of these mental wanderings are presented in a style reminiscent of James Joyce, but what is achieved is a perceptive picture of a rather obnoxious college sophomore who is sophisticated enough to place himself at some distance from his surroundings. For him, abstraction and intellection are fun—a game to be enjoyed; but such ways of passing his time do not prepare the young narrator for the encounter which those in the car face in the midst of the desert. In the broiling heat, abandoned and alone, a Negro is seen standing at the side of the road; but the car does not stop to help him. Many excuses by both husband and wife follow; but what is especially significant is that one sees the narrator (and certainly the young Agee too) perceive, as in a flash, that no abstraction can cope with such an encounter. The experience is so moving that the narrator is forced to break the flow of his prose into a rhetorical pattern of "It was thus. . . . It was thus. . . . It was thus . . . ," to relate how each person reacted to that particular human being in need. Words alone, and certainly no amount of sophistication or abstraction, can suggest the complexity of such a situation. The narrator says: "In purely abstract argument I had talked myself red-eyed and ready for murder, on this matter of the Negro and his place; and now, when I was involved in actuality, I could say nothing and do nothing."[33]

As Agee encountered the complexity of the world, he began to realize that he could not intellectualize without losing the immediacy of experience. When one looks at the whole of his literary career, minute areas of experience, such as the encounter described in "Death in the Desert," became of greatest value for him as subjects about which to write. Interestingly, much of this writing resulted in poetry of which some of the lyrical passages in *Famous Men* ("On the Porch," "A Country Letter") are illustrative. Although one might describe this development in method as a dislike of abstraction, Agee sought ways to write which would falsify as little as possible. His respect for the quotidian brought about a change in emphasis.

Agee came to realize that the "actual" was a series of moments which flowed together to provide a texture unique in itself. The analogy between apprehension and the film is obvious. While an undergraduate he surely was thinking about the mechanics of motion pictures, and the relationship of this to the process of thinking. The narrator of "Death in the Desert" thus can recall childhood experiences in Tennessee; and, because a certain event "was very fine," he could run "it through now two or three times" to get the full effect of the remembrance. How to verbalize such remembrance remained, as has been observed, a dilemma for Agee.

In another Harvard story, "They That Sow in Sorrow Shall Reap," Agee took an ordinary experience and attempted to catch its rhythm;[34] and this effort is the best anticipation of his mature writing. The narrator lives in a bordinghouse operated by an old couple, and his story is an attempt to evoke the complexity of a particular moment as supported by a web of events which led up to and through that moment. At the base of the story is the narrator's realization that there is no way to control one's involvement in the reality of being with, and interacting with, other persons. Just as in "Death in the Desert" when the automobile passes a man, and the emotional involvement of the moment overpowers the narrator's ability to order his thoughts, in "They That Sow . . ." a basic fact communicated is the realization that all persons are subject to forces that are not fully explicable. A pitiable old man makes vague homosexual gestures toward the narrator and another young man; but, while the old man is terribly lonely and radiates a mildly sinister appearance, he is a person who "showed only gentleness and kindliness, and embarrassing humility. . . ." The narrator, as he witnesses the results of the old man's actions, is less concerned for himself than for the others who live in the boardinghouse. The result of the action has been an embarrassment not just for the old man and his strangely loyal wife, but for all those who were intricately bound up in the household.

But the narrator is primarily fascinated with the difficulty of catching the rhythm of this experience; he confesses that it is impossible to catch its complexity; and some of his doubts about what he was doing are reflected in the following statement: "I suppose the essentials of which this music is compounded are the facts as they are, tempered by sternness and pity and calm. We are eight people in this house; we are endowed with as many different minds, or souls, and with as many different machines for attacking existence, and defending ourselves against it." The statement echoes ideas of I. A. Richards, whom Agee had met at Harvard and greatly admired, but it also reflects Agee's awareness of the complexity of the way in which any moment is compounded of the interaction of multitudinous elements, as well as by the fact that an artist cannot place himself fully within the consciousness of another. Each person lives, the narrator suggests, "dimly in the center of being, and thence we perform the most ordinary duties, and avoid others; to some extent we guide our lives, to some extent are guided by them; and the whole object of life, whatever it may or should be, is hidden beyond a profound and inescapable confusion of egoism and of altruism and of evil and of good." Despite this complaint, the rhythm of an action is caught; and Agee foreshadows a method sustained later in *Famous Men*.

Agee's capabilities are, therefore, most in evidence in his undergraduate fiction when the distance between writer and his subject matter are minimal. He seems not to have fully realized, however, that his talent was best suited for such a personal evocation of actuality. Much of his undergraduate writing reflects an artist who sought ways of making religious and philosophical beliefs meaningful.

III   *Toward Freer Forms*

Agee's writing after he left Harvard is characterized by more frequent employment of freer forms, and this development was paralleled by changes within him. Apparently he experienced a waning of interest in explicitly religious subjects, and he began to express concern with a more immediate apprehension of reality. He realized that the world offered an abundance of poetic material, and he sought appropriate methods to project his apprehension of that actuality. Because the "low dishonest decade" in which he matured was a time of disillusionment, Agee's Christianity, as well as his hopes to become a writer, seemed of little consequence during an era that pulsated with economic problems. Often his Harvard writing reflected a confidence in Christianity and indicated his hope to interweave religious faith into his post-Harvard writing. But the later poems which deal with religion often convey the impression that he could not find a suitable means to express belief. Or, perhaps he felt religion was largely meaningless for modern America. In "A Chorale," included in *Permit me Voyage* he sang:

> O Godsent Son of God our allsalvation,
> ....
> Your faith who gave your heart for our safekeeping,
> Your love who sweated blood while we were sleeping,
> If so these waste within this generation
> > Death is your nation:
> The time is withered of your ancient glory:
> Your doing in this dear earth a pretty story:
> O noblest heart fare well through the conclusion
> > Of all delusion.[35]

Peter Ohlin explains that, while the "choice of genre is . . . symptomatic of Agee's strong commitment to his religious background . . . [,] the poem remains too strongly bound by its own archaism to be quite effective."[36] This statement seems to mean effectiveness for a large audience, but no such audience existed. If Agee were to find an audience, he had to do so through use of less orthodox subjects.

Agee himself wrote that he considered *Permit Me Voyage* to be a record of past accomplishments. By the time it appeared two years after he had arrived in New York as a staff writer for *Fortune* magazine, his mind was teeming with other kinds of writing projects. He already had rejected the idea of publishing a collection of short stories, and he was still at work on the ambitious poem "John Carter." *Permit Me Voyage*, when published, reflected the range of his poetic skill, but it only hinted at what he was later to accomplish.

At no point in his career was Agee ever classifiable within a movement or by an ideology. Perhaps this fact is truest of the time in the mid-1930s when his first book, and only collection of poetry, was published. Agee's own "Reflections on Permit Me Voyage," an unpublished commentary about the book, indicates the many types of writing which he produced during the early 1930s. He noted that putting *Permit Me Voyage* together was a "good deal of trouble" because, if he had used everything which he had written, it "would jangle, more than even I could care for." He specifically mentions "John Carter," "pieces of a play," and "an outlandish Radio Poem," as other possibilities for a first volume.[37] Thus his first book might well have been far different in content than it actually was.

IV *Permit Me Voyage*

Permit Me Voyage can best be described as a collection of technical exercises accumulated in attempts to find a suitable voice. Among the poems in this volume are the ten opening lyrics; an "Epithalamium" done in the manner of Spenser; "Ann Garner," the long narrative poem written at Exeter; a sonnet sequence reminiscent of the Elizabethans; and "A Chorale." At times, the poems possess an unusual juxtaposition between statement and format; yet Agee appears to have desired the traditional more than the innovative. The only radically different poem in the volume is "Dedication," a prose-poem catalogue. The book was well received by reviewers, but some of them felt that Agee might have taken more pains to remove himself from the poems. The critical comments generally reflected approval of the technical competence of the poems and hopes were expressed about Agee's promise.[38]

Basic to *Permit Me Voyage* is its variation of style, for the volume contains poetry ranging from Shakespearean sonnets to a flowing prose poem which echoes Walt Whitman and W. H. Auden. The opening lyrics once again include the *carpe diem* theme, but their language is that of a near-conversational mode. Ohlin suggests that the "sexuality implicit in the images is, just as in some seventeenth-century poetry, controlled by the grace and ceremony of the presentation,"[39] but something beyond imitation is accomplished in the opening set of lyrics. In his unpublished commentary, Agee states that the lyrics are "all attempts to swing Elizabethan spontaneity into contemporary uses." Such experimentation had not been manifest in his undergraduate poems in which the language usually remained conventional, and attempts to fuse the traditional with contemporary usage were not common in the undergraduate poems. Thus, the form and attitude of implied criticism reflected in "Good Friday," in which the crucifixion of Christ is also the death of Pan, is predictable. Man's encounter with the world was changed by Christ's action: Pan "hears the strokes/ Of iron on iron, and his own hooves/ The iron strikes through."[40] A closeness with nature was lost with the crucifixion; and that loss affects man's spontaneity of action.

"Good Friday" is not so successful a presentation of ideas about spontaneity as is an opening poem of *Permit Me Voyage*, "The Happy Hen":

> His hottest love and most delight
> The rooster knows for speed of fear
> And winds her down and treads her right
> And leaves her stuffed with dazzled cheer,
>
> Rumpled allwhichways in her lint,
> Who swears, shrugs, redeems her face,
> And serves to mind us how a sprint
> Heads swiftliest for the state of grace. (7)

This lyric (also a satire of a marriage manual) suggests that spontaneity may be the most advantageous preparation for eternal life. The word "redeems" is not used accidentally nor is the phrase "state of grace" which ends it. This lyric indirectly reminds one that an engagement with actuality may be more satisfactory than any theorizing.

Common to many of the opening lyrics is an expressed pity that man is forced to suffer. Thus a child's death is to be celebrated because, while as fragile as the smallest leaf, it was "Not met and marred with the year's whole turn of grief./ But easily in the mercy of the morning/ Fell this still folded leaf." Other lyrics are more reflective, and "Description of Elysium" ironically suggests that man's sorrow is often the result of reflectiveness. The paradise of Elysium cannot be possessed by man:

> No thing is there thinks:
> Mind the witherer
> Withers on the outward air:
> We can not come there. (6)

All of Agee's lyrics are carefully crafted. "Sure on this shining night,"a moment of arrested awareness, was later set to music by Samuel Barber. Another lyric evokes the moment of recognition when love's absence is felt, but the speaker realizes that all is not over: "The dog returns. And the man to his mother./ And tides. And you to me. And I to you." These lovers are

> . . . cowardly kind the cruellest way,
> Feeling the cliff unmorsel from our heels
> And knowing balance gone, we smile, and stay
> A little, whirling our arms like desperate wheels. (4)

These concluding lines imply an awareness of the difficulty of sustaining any human relationship, and they indicate the futility of not accepting the paradoxical situation of men. Little good comes from whirling arms like a foolish mechanical contrivance. Man must submit; yet, even if all things are in constant flux, from time to time the rhythm of earth's beauty is felt.

Still another opening lyric suggests much of what informs the whole book: a playfulness and an awareness of the certainty of death are combined with the urge to accept life. This lyric, "Child, should any pleasant boy," addressed to a "child" pleads for her not to be coy with "the sly delays of maidenhood." "Since soon, too soon, the wolfer night/ Climbs in between, and ends fair play." In all of the lyrics, Agee insists upon the cyclical nature of earthly activities; for all beauty and joy fade; and change "soon, too soon" "ends fair play." In another of these lyrics a speaker states that the summer sun stunned him "full of waking sleep" and in a dream he lingered with thoughts of the future. But night came: "The shade o'erswam me like a sheet/ Of draughty disappointed vans,/ And lobbered beak, and drawling feet." The day, the brightness, life are short. This poem, with its emphasis on the disappointments of the dreamer, should be related to Agee's later writing, for the harsh awakening of the dreamer is a recurrent idea in *Famous Men*.

The most important poem in the book is the unique prose poem "Dedication," which, in Agee's words, is "not of the lousy volume, as any fool should know, but of all I am or can be: to God, to truth, and to art which is both." In relation to his later work as a journalist and as a poet, this poem is invaluable. It is an experiment in structure; a catalogue of items loved (and hated); and a prayer. The famous and unknown, artists and artisans are praised in "Dedication" which begins

> *in much humility*
> *to God in the highest*
> *in the trust that he despises nothing*

> *And in his commonwealth:*

To those who in all times have sought truth
and who have told it in their art or in their
living, who died in honor; and chiefly to these:
Christ: Dante: Mozart: Shakespeare: [etc.] Van Gogh:
and to an unknown sculptor of China, for his
god's head.
....

To those who in their living time were frustrate
with circumstance, and disadvantage; to those who
died in the still desire of truth who never knew
truth, nor much beauty, and small joy but the goodness of endurance; to all those who in all times
have labored in the earth and who have wrought their
time blindly, patient in the sun: and to all the
dead in their generations: (8—9)

Agee acknowledges that the past cannot be ignored while the present is accepted. His catalogue of events and persons is an indication of his realization that everything, no matter how contradictory, is worthy of attention. And so among those to whom he dedicated himself were " . . . men who, of all nations unhindered, to all nations faithless, make it their business to destroy concord and to incite war and to prolong it, for their profit . . . "; but he was also quick to add: "To those who think that any, or much, or all this condition may be a little, or much, or wholly changed. And to those who think that any one man is wholly guilty."

"Dedication" is an attempt to fuse an Anglo-Catholic heritage and love of God with an acceptance of the contemporary world.[41] As a catalogue of what Agee felt important for artistic and intellectual development, the poem includes a listing of the living and dead who influenced him; obliquely outlines subjects which Agee feels are of importance, such as use of the American idiom; reflects the complexity of an existence immensely complicated by the constant presence of both good and evil; sings the praise of God; and, finally, sings of the world as it is without hope for change, or cure. "Dedication" ends with a prayer—in the formal sense: "O God, hear us/ O God, spare us./ O God, have mercy upon us"—but the complete poem is a prayer, and the spirit of prayer informs the volume as a whole. This poetry is for God in a darkened time.

A year after the publication of *Permit Me Voyage*, Agee could still write that God was present in his world, but His presense was less than glorious:

> Death paid and living earned he walks
> The spirals of our present hell.
> Steep on whose terrific street
> Shines the calmness of his feet.
> Sulphurous around him glare
> The maledictions of despair.[42]

The 1930s were debilitating when compared with earlier ages of belief, for America seemed at a low point. One of Agee's most successful expressions of this fact is "A Chorale," the poem which is the centerpiece of *Permit Me Voyage;* a song of praise to God, it is also a plea: "Dear Christ awaken;" "See now sweet farmer what a wasting shadow/ Takes your green meadow" (27). In this work, rhythm and rhyme unite to suggest what has been lost with the passing of religious belief.

Agee's own "Reflections" about "A Chorale" provide insight into this central poem. He noted that religion, "though an artifice, was a clearer lens than I had yet polished, and . . . the clearest of which I had any knowledge was the Catholic Church. So, elsewhere and in this poem particularly, that church was used. This limited the poem, as all symbols must: it also helped give it skeleton, and clarity. Religion is not, after all, utterly irrelevant to God. . . ." Robert Fitzgerald, who comments on Agee's poetic reliance upon tradition, notes that "Chorale" is "in direct line of descent from English achievements of the period between 1550 and 1640"; yet it is wrong to consider it imitative because meaning is added to tradition.[43] Agee's poem is a lament for the absence of God. J. Douglas Perry points to the success of the poem when he writes "it is not simply disgust at man's behavior that makes the tone . . . modern. It is the implied fear that God may truly have been weakened by man's neglect."[44]

Two other long poems in this volume are adaptations of techniques which seem less suited to Agee's temperament. "Epithalamium", written in 1930, is quite different from its model, Spenser's of the same name; and, while the two poems need not be compared, their difference is significant. Spenser's speaker sings of his happiness and marriage: "Behold how goodly my faire loue does ly/ In proud humility. . . ." Agee's speaker remains on the perimeter, uninvolved in the action, and his poem seems less joyful than Spenser's. The diction and rhythms are successful; yet the circumlocutions and euphemisms of Agee's poem contribute to a stilted effect. Passages such as "Quiet on her bed amid the glancing dews,/ Queenly she waits in rich humility" are beautiful; but other lines seem inappropriately indirect: "Knotted in secrecy, the sacred zone/ From every harm the unharmed virgin shields." Moreover, too much emphasis is placed upon the sexual act itself; in contrast, Spenser's poem is broader in intent, treatment, and result. Agee seems to write of an intellectualized mystery, and Perry argues that Agee's poem does not present "the masque or pageant of a bridal procession" but is, instead, "a reflective journey undertaken by a member of the wedding party. . . . intensely aware of an imperfect world, and aware that it is man who largely makes it so." The poem can be profitably read in this spirit.[45]

"Ann Garner," another narrative poem, predates "Epithalamium," having been composed at Exeter in 1928; Horace Gregory found this poem the worst of the volume.[46] Minor revisions were made, but a lack of immediacy leaves the poem rather abstract, even though effective phrases and insights combine to make the union of Ann with death a substantial achievement for an eighteen year old. The poem attempts to picture a wide span of years, and it unfortunately lacks coherence. "Ann Garner" is the chronicle of a mountain woman who bears a dead child, and must then carry the grief of that death. She slowly becomes a kind of earth-mother, and her own death comes in an open field above the grave of her child. She uses her sorrow for her lost child as a means to build toward a realization that death brings cosmic life.

Such an outline does injustice to a poem which contains many individually good images; but the poem is as cold as the dead Ann Garner herself. The reader sees that she "never would have died within four walls," and that God "sows the universe anew"; but the reader is not fully convinced by the ritualistic horrors which Agee includes—the details of death and burial by her husband are contrived. "Ann Garner" appears to have been influenced by the themes and diction of both E. A. Robinson and Robinson Jeffers, and perhaps Robert Frost.[47] The poem is a sustained demonstration of technical competence, but, above all, an exercise; and Agee may have retained "Ann Garner" because it reflected "the ambition of [an] attempt at narrative with variations, not really like Jeffers but reaching like him toward myth, a vision of elemental life in the American earth."[48]

The most skillful poems in the book are the twenty-five sonnets which combine an awareness of the difficulty of writing along with a confrontation of man's mortality that reminds the reader of man's frailty "fashioned on a chain of flesh." While the links of those "ancient lengths are immolate in dust," the fate of the poet is to strive against mortality. To be reminded of frailty and to accept the challenge of writing are the speaker's difference from those who preceded him and also his source of life: " 'Tis mine to touch with deathlessness their clay:/ And I shall fail, and join those I betray." Man cannot be satisfied in his finite nature:

> Our doom is in our being. We began
> In hunger eager more than ache of hell:
> And in that hunger became each a man
> Ravened with hunger death alone may spell: (37)

The use of language is reassuring. Connections with antecedents can be verbalized: "we" live "as lived the dead," and know even love "is as the grass." "And all the goodliness of love the flower/ Of grass . . . its little day shall pass."

Thematically, the sonnets resemble later autobiographical

writing. Sonnet XXIII, typical of the sequence and much later work
too, focuses on an awareness of life, "the breath and bulk of being,"
met now in a speaker who "from the eldest shade/ Of all un-
dreamt" was raised into seeing. Present vision "is compacted from
"sense and dream and death." The speaker realizes that he will
never know much of the wisdom which preceded his being, and
thus will never be able to make poetry of that wisdom. This same
mood informs the later fragment "Now as Awareness. . . ."

Many of the sonnets center on the poet's vocation. The last unites
a reflection of hopes for a poetic career, along with the realization of
how the career must be within a troubled time.

> My sovereign souls, God grant my sometime brothers,
> I must desert your ways now if I can.
> I followed hard but now forsake all others,
> And stand in hope to make myself a man.
> This mouth that blabbed so loud with foreign song
> I'll shut awhile, or gargle if I sing.
> Have patience, let me too, though it be long
> Or never, till my throat shall truly ring.
>
> These are confusing times and dazed with fate:
> Fear, easy faith, or wrath's on every voice:
> Those toward the truth with brain are blind or hate:
> The heart is cloven on a hidden choice:
> In which respect I still shall follow you.
> And, when I fail, know where the fault is due. (49)

Acceptance of the poet's role is guarded. Agee knew that his ap-
prenticeship was past and that he would have to write alone, since
his phrase "foreign song" seems to indicate that he realizes he must
find his own voice.

The concluding poem, "Permit Me Voyage," is an acceptance of
the poet's role and an expression of hope to "herald" God. The concluding line is from Hart Crane's "Voyage III:" "Permit me
voyage, love, into your hands." The speaker implies that man will
be preserved through poetry. To God, he speaks: "I know" how
"The crested glory is declined:" but "True poets shall walk who
herald you:/ Of whom God grant me of your grace/ To be, that
shall preserve this race." Agee's remark, made during the last year

of his life, that he was born to write poetry is recalled; but little could he realize so early in his career that much of his poetry was to be done in prose. Yet he certainly sensed that *Permit Me Voyage* marked a completed stage in his career. He noted retrospectively that his final decision had been to "put into the book such things as seem to me, for one reason or another, finished, crystallized, behind me."[49] In fact, most of the traditional poetry which he wrote was accomplished when the book appeared in 1934.

V   *"Theme with Variations"*

A poem which Fitzgerald dates as approximately 1933, "Theme with Variations," demonstrates a transition from the derivative quality of much of *Permit Me Voyage* to a later poetic manner, one that is often more experimental.[50] Its theme, the beauty of sleep and the coming of night—a cyclical movement—centers on the constant need for change and renewal: "Through all the shadow's scope/ The dew distends its tide." Agee himself remarked that this poem was one of his favorites. Its seemingly simple subject demanded a complex method, and "Theme with Variations" presents its subject with the intricacy of musical forms. The rhythm of its opening section employs "alternate elision or extension of pauses which suggests the continual play of rotating rhythm and universe."[51] The quatrains provide an image of the coming of night, a resemblance to death, but a change and a renewal, which bring wholeness. Through the coming of night, creatures and the world itself can continue. The movement of the opening section suggests the cyclical movement: "Night stands up the east" and concludes "And up the east fares day."

The variations which follow trace the poet's awareness of approaching night, its peacefulness, and its effects upon different creatures. Sleep, as an experience of human kind, is the subject of the second poem: "All pomp of day put from you/ And deep through darkness bow." The first variation reminds the reader that man cannot get far away from his origins, his animal needs, and his realization that death remains close at hand.

The tone of "Variation 2" is light and playful. This poem is a listing and elaboration of the many beasts which also must submit to sleep and the renewal of night.

> Sourbrained mule and horse meekheaded
> Grimbutted cow and dafteyed sheep
> Gristly hog and their gay children
> All have shut them whole in sleep [.]

The following variation moves further downward in the evolutionary scale; the subject is the myriads of birds who have sung and flown throughout the day: "The eagerest wing that was abroad/ Is idle now and the wing outlawed." The final variation takes still another step back as lizards and insects and bees are contemplated. Throughout, specific images suggest the universality of sleep for all.

"Theme with Variations" presents a vision of sleep and of night which brings renewal. The reader is reminded of the mystery that man must, like all creatures, submit to things which essentially he can never understand. Agee celebrates this mystery with a combination of precise images and a rhythm which suggests the simplicity of something as unremarkable as sleep. These variations, an experiment in sound, were not published during Agee's lifetime because he had not completed the variations on day. He did, however, record the poem;[52] and his recitation from memory indicates his fondness for it. Such themes of the transience of man and the cyclical nature of the universe's renewal support much of Agee's writing. Those ideas, interwoven throughout *Permit Me Voyage*, became the core of Agee's tenant book. But, before that prose was written, Agee was to experiment with still other kinds of writing.

CHAPTER 3

The Thirties

I *Distractions as Journalist*

W HEN Agee was graduated from Harvard, he sensed he could
be a competent writer; but he also realized that he should
develop new modes of writing, and much of what he accomplished
in the 1930s developed through this awareness. His undated poem
of regular quatrains, "You Green in the Young Day," apparently
written in the mid-1930s, again utilizes the theme of cyclical change
that was used heavily in the undergraduate poetry; but the poem is
private, and reflects an awareness that for him expression in conventional poetic ways seemed unsatisfactory. The final lines conclude
with the plea:

> And so may this ill-tuned remark
> Of mine, and many others,
> Run light among the living
> When I am in the dark.[1]

Going to New York to work at *Fortune* may have promised to be
an adventure in 1932; and falling in love and marrying in 1933 must
have been a happy time. But it was not long before the pressures of
a job which consumed most of his energy, along with the difficulties
of a melancholy temperament and of marriage, began to impinge
painfully upon his consciousness. Two sonnets, the first dated 1933,
delineate some of the difficulties he apparently experienced. The
first is a love poem about "two fragments found to fit entire" that
are haunted by the awareness that dreams cannot be fulfilled. The
companion poem written about two years later, begins:

54

Two years have passed, and made a perfect wheel
Of all that we can know of joy and pain.
All that lovers hope or dread to feel
We've felt, and are arrived at naught again.[2]

Such circular movement of emotion had already been established as
a predominant theme in Agee's work; but these sonnets emphasize
personal disappointment.

During his first years in New York, he wrote at least twice to
Father Flye to explain that he was depressed, was even in a suicidal
frame of mind. In October, 1933, he explained that he would stay
on as a writer for *Fortune*, "But Lord knows with misgiv-
ings . . . no earthly thing is as important to me as learning how
to write and for that you *must* have time!" Such frustration, in combination with what Agee himself once described as "a hideous trait
of moodiness", made his earliest years in New York less productive
than later ones of the decade.[3] But some writing was accomplished:
Permit Me Voyage appeared; other poems were written; and most
importantly, plans were made for other projects with word and image. The position as journalist for *Fortune* helped him to formulate
his theoretical base for new types of writing.

When, for instance, Agee was given an assignment to write about
a modern interior, he commented that decorators themselves were
probably unaware of what a "modern" interior could be; therefore,
his assignment was both instructive and frustrating: "About like being assigned to do an article on aerodynamics and having to illustrate it with pictures of streamlined fountain-pens . . . with one
airplane tossed in as an afterthought."[4] Dwight Macdonald recalls
that Agee was regarded as the magazine's specialist in "rich,
beautiful prose"; and Agee's journalistic writing does at times seem
to be the work of a frustrated poet.[5] In many places in these un-
signed pieces, Agee's personality clearly informs the style, as is the
case with the prose of "The Drought" and "The Great American
Roadside." In both, an expansiveness of vision and a love of land are
revealed; and, while the articles remain factual, they reveal Agee's
consciousness of the possibilities everywhere available for analysis.

In "The Great American Roadside" the motel industry is chroni-

cled in business-magazine manner; statistics about tourist cottages
and hot-dog stands finally envelop the article; but, in the midst of
abundant factual data, Agee sprinkles sentences which reveal his
enthusiasm. Roadside customs are to be respected, and the satirist
who "lampoons American folkways fails to see that most folkways
make sense." The road itself is to be observed for what it is:
"scraggled and twisted along the coast of Maine . . . in Florida
the detours are bright with the sealime of rolled shells . . . the
road degrades into a lattice of country dirt athwart Kansas . . . like a blacksnake in the sun it takes the ridges, the green
and dim ravines which are the Cumberlands, and rolls loose into the
hot Alabama valleys."[6] Such phrases reflect Agee's respect for actuality.

Similar interests are expressed in other articles which include personal observations. His article about the Tennessee Valley Authority
takes the reader back to the hills of Tennessee and to the small city
of Knoxville to describe how the surrounding area was changing
with the arrival of the Tennessee Valley Authority.[7] Agee includes
examples of people who reaped profits because of changes, and he
even mentions an undertaker near LaFollette who had won a con-
tract to move a number of graves. It is impossible to read that
sentence without remembering the fictional Ralph of A Death in
the Family. Also, occasionally, as in "August at Saratoga," Agee
concentrates on providing accurate images: city streets, deserted,
early in the morning "are as strangely empty as a new-made corpse
of breath . . . and swift and broad, upon the lush elms and the
kaleidoscopic slate shingles and the wild gables and the apoplec-
tically swirled colonnades and the bare porches and the egregiously
extensive and pitiable slums of this little curious city, there
settles . . . the chill and the very temper and the very cold of
death."[8]

Agee wrote at least twenty-five articles for Fortune, but usually
not on subjects which he might have chosen himself. Only with the
chance to go to Alabama in 1936 for a survey of cotton tenantry did
this become the case. He devoted himself to his writing with
assiduousness, however, and he won the approval of Henry Luce,
his editor. For a while, a joke circulated that Henry Luce intended
to send Agee to the Harvard business school.

II *"John Carter"*

Agee, of course, was not interested in becoming a student in any
school of business for he could see little profit in becoming a better
economist if doing so would not help him to be a better writer. He
had little intention of staying on at *Fortune*, and he applied as early
as 1932 for a Guggenheim fellowship with hopes that perhaps its
twenty-five hundred dollar award would support him for a sustained period in France. One of the projects he hoped to finish was a
long poem already underway and entitled "John Carter." Parts of it
had appeared in the *Advocate* in 1932. This unique, but unfinishable poem, continued to hold interest for four more years, but
he stopped working on it in 1936. His editor, Robert Fitzgerald,
makes it clear that Agee may not have desired any of his unfinished
poetry reprinted, but that is not an easy judgment to make about
"John Carter," a poem which Agee said "could be a complete appraisal of contemporary civilization, and a study of the Problem of
Evil."[9] To ignore "John Carter" is especially difficult in view of
Agee's later interest in documentary criteria. Fitzgerald includes it,
therefore, in *The Collected Poems*, because it demonstrates an important and often overlooked facet of Agee's creativity.

In Agee's application for the fellowship in 1932, he listed what he
hoped to accomplish in "John Carter." Among these hopes was the
desire to create poetry which large varieties of people might enjoy,
and his poem was to use idiomatic expressions in its attempt to accomplish for this century what Byron had done for the nineteenth.
He wanted to give contemporary language variety and vitality and
to write poetry which would hold modern attention. A light tone
would, he hoped, not only hold the reader's interest but also enforce
the serious passages and lead the reader to accept a moral and
religious intention. This intent was "to help establish a proper sort
of pride in American civilization," to bring a sense of the dramatic
and narrative vigor usually found only in prose into poetry, and to
help "change the prevalent negative state of mind" to a positive
one. Agee readily admitted he had no idea how long "John Carter"
might be.[10] Thus, innumerable digressions were included, such as
the unplaced stanzas written in December, 1935, and printed in
The Collected Poems, which contain considerations of contemporary historical figures and neocolonialism with stanzas ending:

58

"And thanks to British pluck and the Almighty dollar,/We'll fit the whole round world to a Rhodes collar" (122).

"John Carter" was admittedly an overly ambitious attempt to appraise civilization in *ottava rima*. But, because Agee continued to work on the poem for years, it necessitates attention. "John Carter" generally has been ignored by commentators even when they limit themselves to a discussion of Agee's poetry. While the poem is not so successful as it might be, it has merits as a delineation of contemporary civilization and as an analysis of evil. As always, Agee was aware of cultural complexity; and "Dedication," already examined, echoes "John Carter" and also demonstrates this multiplicity. In conception, "John Carter" is as ambitious as *Famous Men;* but this poem is larger in vision than anything else he attempted. In quantity, it is his most impressive poem and many individual stanzas are good, but those are only fragments.

"John Carter," by its nature, is unfinishable; but, even so, many glimmerings remain of what might have been accomplished. Parts of "John Carter" suggest its grand design, and his working notes about sunrise, which would lead into a presentation of mother and father asleep, provide insight into what Agee wanted to accomplish. The completed twelve stanzas for this section succeed because individuals and the overall design are united. The poem was to be built on a constant need for digression; the reader was to be frequently reminded of Carter's imagined history as representative. As sunrise is ended, the speaker returns to specifics, the literal conception of his hero. Agree wrote:

> But of the wide realm of the joyous field
>   With beast and farmer bustling in the grain,
> And of this grimed but sweetly glistering shield
>   And early citizens hustling to their pain—
> Of all this earth that mildly lies revealed
>   To busyness that soon enough shall wane,
> Of Asia reeling upward toward the dawn,
>   No more: return to our heroic spawn. (93)

The stanzas surrounding the description of sunrise are contemplative. Agee sings of how "Over one badge of city on broad ground/A breathing silver brightens and is day." Morning comes surrounded with sounds: "music of bird," "scythe on wheat," "Of startled engines and a million feet." Such phrases and lines reveal Agee's ability to stand back from contemporary civilization.

Agee wanted to make "a complete appraisal of contemporary civilization," but only two long sections were completed along with various unplaced stanzas. As Fitzgerald notes, "Jim's fairly savage examination of certain Episcopalian attitudes and decor—and even more, the sheer amount of this—indicates quite adequately how 'Church' and 'organized religion' in relation to awe and vision, bothered his mind." Such satire directed against the church receives maximum treatment, and the description of the hero's baptismal church is typical; its architecture and art work, "pretty chic/compared to those cockeyed asymmetries/which peasants labored up for centuries." Agee's satire attacks the complexity of a society which seems to have lost any reverence for tradition, and much of the poem emphasizes the hypocrisy and deceit which inform much high-church Episcopalianism. Even its architecture is false, an import of something which long ago faded in England. The main concern of the architect for the church where young Carter is baptized was that its appearance be externally proper, and such external propriety is at the heart of much of modern religion and living—and such superficialty amused Agee. Modern technology provides the appearance of churchiness with practically none of the earlier centuries of effort:

> The tower and all that blocky church was cool,
>> Spat-colored stone, perfectly joined and sleek,
> Scored with the breath of every rapid tool
>> That shaved and manicured it in a week. (116)

Agee attacks his age; religion is clothed in attractive dress, so attractive that finally externals are without meaning. The altar is so nicely done in marble that finally all that is needed "is spiggots to suggest a bath."

American attitudes toward business, advertising, and sex are also objects of Agee's attention. Usually his attack is presented through an amalgam of American language, especially in the case of sex. Agee combines cliché, advertising jargon, and parody in hilarious combinations, as in digressions about Leonard Dash:

True lust will triumph over indigestion:
(God moves in a mysterious way, I hear,
But here and now I think we'd really best shun
Such thoughts, and say biology is queer) (87)

In "John Carter," written so that it will constantly entertain,
Agee demonstrated with his completed stanzas that poetry might be
written for a wide audience. His digression about the defects of
babies is indicative of the kind of success which might have been
achieved had he been able to sustain more interest in "John
Carter." After a few stanzas outlining the more undesirable
characteristics of babies, the speaker announces he must stop: "You
can look up their other worse defects"; but, of course, he does not
stop at all. The next stanza begins: "And I'd suggest you start in
with the lung." By the end of the following stanza, he has reversed
himself to suggest: "If I could have my own exclusive baby,/Maybe
I'd like him rather more than maybe." Then, of course, there are
other reversals in following passages.

Above all, "John Carter" stands as an indication of vast ambition.
The poem is certain evidence that much energy and enthusiasm
were devoted to projects other than his writing for *Fortune*. When
he applied for the Guggenheim Fellowship in 1932, however, he
knowingly indicated to Father Flye that little chance existed to win
one because he was not an established writer and that, therefore, he
must try to get as much accepted by magazines as possible. He
knew "John Carter" stood little chance of successful completion;
and unfortunately, except for *Permit Me Voyage*, little was published during the next five years. But, by 1937, when he again applied
for a Guggenheim, he had published some poems; and several years
of experimentation and frustration seem to have helped him
because he had moved toward creation of freer forms. He had taken
a leave from *Fortune* for six months in 1935–1936, and by 1937 he
was bubbling over with ideas about how he could write, collect, and
analyze. His hopes and plans, surprisingly unconventional from any
ordinary point of view, are much closer to what he later accomplished than his hopes expressed five years earlier for "John
Carter."

III *"Plans for Work"*

"Plans for Work: October 1937," which accompanied his second application for a Guggenheim Fellowship, included an outline for forty-seven separate proposed projects. They range from suggestions about how he might develop "An Alabama Record" for the recording of information gathered during six thousand miles of travel during the summer of 1936 to statements about various pieces of fiction, notes on photography, music, theater, and revues.[11] At least five of the projects are suggestions for fiction; but, significantly, Agee also wished to write stories "whose whole intention is the direct communication of the intensity of common experience." Far outweighing any concern with traditional forms of writing are suggestions such as the following:

A *"new" style of use of the imagination.*
   In the Alabama record the effort is to suspect the mind of invention and to invent nothing. But another form of relative truth is any person's imagination of what he knows little or nothing of and has never seen. . . .

City streets. Hotel Rooms. Cities.
   And many other categories. Again, the wish is to consider such *in their own terms*, not as decoration or atmosphere for fiction.

Analyses of miscommunication; the corruption of ideas.
   . . . every first-rate idea and most discoveries of fact, move and become degraded and misused against their own ends.

These elaborate proposals contain outlines for various kinds of analysis, poetry, and collection of data; in fact, enough is suggested to keep scores of writers busy for many years. Most of the plans are only ideas, but they reflect Agee as he overflowed with hopes to examine how men see or fail to see their world. These plans best illustrate his turning away from conventional writing. He had earlier entertained the possibility of publishing a collection of fiction, but the 1937 plans represent a turning away from the conventional forms of "Art" and a movement toward the world itself. For such reasons, within several of his categories, Agee's hopes for the camera, both still and motion, are included. His hope for a new kind of film, akin to the lyric poem, is only now beginning to be explored some thirty years after its suggestion.

A predominant idea found in many of the proposals emphasizes a need for methods to analyze everyday realities. Agee saw that a tremendous amount could be learned from a collection and analysis of letters, photographs, or public comments. He saw that court records and newspaper columns were as revealing as self-indictments. He argued that a record of a street or a room "in its own terms" has a distinct value different from its use as atmosphere in a work of fiction. He was fascinated with the possibilities which the ordinary world offered for analysis and as a challenge to communication. These multifaceted plans had been developing over a long period of time; and, because these many ideas were simmering, the chance to write a study of tenant farming became an excellent avenue for experimentation.

Much of what Agee accomplished in the 1930s is an extension of his fascination with the complexity of ordinary emotion, experience, and consciousness. He knew that there were many critical projects which had never been attempted. He asked, for instance, could fictional methods be used in conjunction with analysis of the "pathology of 'laziness' "? Such an account might include "fear, ignorance, sex misinterpretation and economics" as contributing factors. Or why not write, he inquired, a "new type of 'horror' story" about the horror "that can come of objects and their relationships." Such stories would communicate the intensity of common experience and would concentrate "on what the senses receive and the memory and context does with it." Many of these proposals seem the logical outgrowth of what had already been observed as early as "They That Sow . . ."; they are steps in a progression toward *Famous Men.* Other writing of the middle and late 1930s—scenarios, poetry, and prose—demonstrates how Agee moved from insight to accomplishment.

IV   *Dreams for Screenplays*

The two screenplays written during this decade are heavily reliant on the descriptive. Little dialogue is provided, and a severe, controlled use of sound is employed in *Man's Fate.* In the other screenplay, *The House,* suggested uses of sound are carefully limited to support visual emphases. Agee, as if frustrated by conventional uses of language, sought an extreme means to demonstrate his vision.

Each of these early screenplays is a success as outlined, even though never produced. *Man's Fate*, an adaptation from the André Malraux novel, was published in 1939; and it seems to be essentially an attempt to suggest what could be done with documentary techniques. In accompanying notes, Agee wrote: "All the film should be grainy, hard black and white, flat focus. . . . No smoothness and never luminous. It should not seem to be fiction."[12] That this adaptation was successful has been confirmed by Fitzgerald who relates that Malraux, "who thought he had got everything out of [the] scene, thought again when he read the Agee script."[13] *Man's Fate* uses the episode from Malraux's novel in which Chinese Communists are waiting to be thrown to their deaths in the boiler of a locomotive.

The script, technically, looks forward to the way Agee adapted the literary works of Stephen Crane and others for scenarios a decade later; however, more than just adaptation is of the essence. Agee knew that a precise use of motion picture technique would be necessary, including stop-shots, silence, and careful focus. The concentration was to be on just a few prisoners, and various timbres of a locomotive whistle would be used to heighten effect. Each of these techniques reenforce mood so that a proper apprehension is made of the horror of execution. As this sketch progresses toward the execution, Agee includes suggestions for the use of newsreel shots which would have been satirically juxtaposed with the horror of what was happening: "Swift shot (from newsreel) of Chiang Kai-Shek at desk lifting his face in a Methodist smile as if hearing a pleasant item of conversation." The principal thing which strikes a reader of *Man's Fate* is Agee's attempt to suggest a means of communication without the intermediary of language.

The House, written some two years before the Malraux adaptation, is an even better example of Agee's emphasis on the visual and shows ways to utilize the subjective. On the surface, this scenario seems to be essentially political; but it is, in fact, a mixture of the political and the near-biographical. Set in a small town ("say Knoxville or Chattanooga, Tenn."), this ambitious script functions like symbolic poetry, and what it attempts to communicate remains mysterious. The passing of an older order, Victorian standards, and changes in morality seem to be at the base of Agee's concern.[14] His projected film was to open with an aerial view of the city; then its focus would be on a near-deserted street occupied by a legless pencil vendor and traversed by two sinister looking nuns. Then a group of what at first seem to be boy scouts appears, and this sequence is quickly followed "with swift intimate detail" by shots of "childish feet grinding faces of Negroes, Jews," followed quickly by many other acts of violence including the crucifixion of a handless and footless woman labeled "MOTHER." When it is then made clear that the "Boy Scouts" are adult midgets, a swift series of shots follow of a midget financier, midget war orator, and then midget mothers and sweethearts waving flags. The world of this film is run by midgets. But this is only the beginning. Next, Agee imagines a funeral cortege which would fade into an external shot of the house. Its inhabitants are described as they are in the process of leaving. Maid and butler remain long enough to steal the silver. Then, they too depart, and only one old lady is within the house. Time passes; and a storm and flood destroy the house. The last scene is of children at play in the wreckage. The film was to end in darkness.

This montage of scenes, like so many other things written by Agee, suggests the cyclical nature of life and the encroachment of evil or innocence. Everything changes; everything passes. But more importantly what had been considered respectable (the mores and values of the preceding generation) is demonstrated to be evil. The inhabitants of this "House," ironically, are not destroyed; they only retire momentarily to their car; and a hint is provided that they will return.

Agee's method is, as Ohlin has pointed out, an amalgamation of many different techniques current in the 1930s in conjunction with an imaginative use of visual impressions.[15] Over and over the apparently innocent or ordinary takes on a shocking or surprising overtone when viewed through the lens of the camera. Scenes melt into one another, and the house finally begins to melt back into the ground. Although *The House* seems to be about the disintegration of an old order and about the hypocrisy its façade covers, it also is an experiment with images which reveals states of mind. The house resembles Agee's own grandfather's house, and the imagined film reflects Agee's disappointment with his own family. In fact, one of the occupants of the house, a young man, "everything about him like a barely retained explosion," bears a physical resemblance to

Agee himself. Just as his satiric "Form-letter 7G3" of 1934 is an at-tack upon the combined arts of mortuary science and advertising, *The House* sketches ways to employ a camera to see what might be ordinarily overlooked. Behind the façade is evil, a dishonesty which is to be exposed.

Somewhat the same intent underlies another proposed project during this period, that of writing a parody of an entire issue of the *World-Telegram* "with every news item and ad heightened in its own style. . . ."[16] All such projects—completed or imagined—in-dicate that Agee was learning that he must find ways to catch the reality of his world with freer and more experimental forms than traditional prose or poetic methods. Some of his poetry which appeared in the years after 1934 also demonstrates this change.

V   *New Poetic Forms*

Of the several types of fugitive writing by Agee that appear dur-ing this period, some is clever parody and criticism of society; other poetry is experimental; but the best of this transitional writing is of a personal nature. His "Lyric" which begins "From now on kill America out of your mind," published in *Common Sense* in 1937, seems almost a set of instructions for his better work during these years. Its speaker says that little is to be gained from thinking about abstractions associated with the nation. To think of individuals and "the land/ Mutually shapen as a child of love" is far better.[17]

The lyric "Vertigral," which begins "Demure morning morning margin . . . ," and establishes a very quiet mood, is an experiment with word music. This Agee poem is the only one clearly derived from the poetry of Gerard Manley Hopkins.[18] But intricate interplay of sound is pursued in many other works of this period, and there is no doubt that Agee had absorbed much of the method of inscape from his reading of Hopkins in Robert Hillyer's versification class at Harvard.

The four poems Fitzgerald groups as "Period Pieces from the Mid-Thirties" reveal other uses of language. In various dialects, the poems poke fun at easy solutions. "Fellow-Traveler" laughs at the superficiality of much leftist political action; "Regionalists, Nationalists," questions the expressions of hope offered by political groups. "Agrarian" is perhaps a satiric approach to the stance of the

Fugitive poet-critics of Nashville; "Georgia Democrat" is an indictment:

> An ah calls awn ivah dipaty, Ku Kluxah an ex so-juh
> To keep dem niggahs in day place till ah gits back to
> Jojuh.[19]

Such humor indirectly reflects a conviction that poetry about political action is of minor significance or is not a subject for serious poetry. Agee must have sensed that his best poetry was to come from his memories.

"Summer Evening," which seems to be based on memories, is a short lyric of three quatrains that evokes an ordinary evening in a small town. Such quiet evenings allow care to be shed, and in such moments hope comes: "Hope can cut the roots of reason:/ And the sorrowful man forget."[20] The poem indicates an imaginative return to a quiet that Agee associated with his childhood. Other poems allowed an imaginative return to the Tennessee that he associated with his father's origins. "In Memory of My Father" is an evocation of an evening's quiet in the hills of rural Tennessee as "the blue night blacks above."[21] This natural, quiet, occurrence suggests man's harmony with the earth; and Agee, who loved to read verse aloud, was becoming concerned with verbal harmony. At night everything is quiet, the countryside is at peace; sounds heard are those of night animals and insects. This moment is of peacefulness when children lie quietly in their beds. The field, actively worked by day is also at rest:

> sweet tended field, now meditate your
> children, child, in your smokesweet quilt, joy in your dreams,
> and father, mother: whose rude hands rest you mutual of the
> flesh: rest in your kind flesh well:
>
> And thou most tender earth:
>
> Lift through this love thy creatures on the light.

This poem foreshadows the contemplative method of *Famous Men*.

The beautifully evocative "Sunday: Outskirts of Knoxville, Tenn." is an even better example of Agee's new writing; and in it

Agee demonstrates how inextricably woven is the "fair and foul" of marriage. This freely constructed work has an irregular pattern of sound and imagery. Its images reflect the pain an adult faces as maturity is gained. Woven within this picture is the poet's hope that innocence and joy, part of any person's initial experience, will not be taken away from the young. Agee shows how lives are quickly filled with pain and trivia; yet this is part of a cycle from innocence to wisdom, and from childhood to death. The poem begins with imagery of idyllic young love "followed by an inventory of the inevitable future that slides by with kaleidoscopic changes." Ideas of the opening are reinforced by its sound pattern, "one of light lyrical emphasis and soft internal end rhyme,"[22] until the ending of the opening section is attained:

> There, in the earliest and chary spring, the dogwood flowers.

> Unharnessed in the friendly sunday air
> By the red brambles, on the river bluffs,
> Clerks and their choices pair.[23]

But to be in love is much like being in a trance. Lovers cannot see what is to follow; the speaker knows that, if they realized what love inevitably brings, they could not accept it; for, in his view, with love comes responsibility, and with responsibility, disappointment.

Love cannot continue in its first simplicity for man loves in a world which constantly changes. The delusion of young lovers must end for

> We that are human cannot hope.
> Our tenderest joys oblige us most
> No chain so cuts the bone; and sweetest silk most shrewdly strangles.

The opening lines possess a flowing, rhythmic quality; but the transition emphasizes a monosyllabic harshness which serves as preparation for the catalogue of suffering that follows. In the maturity of love, one must cope with

> . . . bedfights, silences, woman's pages,
> Sickness of heart before goldlettered doors,
> Stale flesh, hard collars, agony in antiseptic corridors . . . ,

and, in addition, with the reality of death: "Arrangements with morticians to be taken care of by sons in law." From these realities the speaker moves toward affirmation—because in childhood innocence is preserved. Therefore, the last of the images in the series moves away from the monosyllabic, and the ending lines of the poem are reinforced by sounds more like the opening.

The idyllic opening is again suggested. For the innocent, future pain is irrelevant. The last lines of the poem suggest that innocence:

> And, in the empty concrete porch, blown ash
> Grandchildren wandering the betraying sun
>
> Now, on the winsome crumbling shelves of horror
> God show, God blind these children!

Here the poet intercedes with God to protect innocence. "Crumbling" man-made "shelves" is an appropriate and concise image suggesting that the horrors of any generation's construction do pass, much as Agee's catalogue of suffering dissolves into an image of innocent children at play. Elizabeth Drew regards this poem so highly that she discusses it in conjunction with poems by Yeats and Shakespeare, and all of Agee's commentators feel it is a success.

The familiar prose sketch "Knoxville: Summer, 1915" was written at approximately the same time as the Knoxville Sunday poem. This sketch is among the best prose of Agee. In contrast to the poem, in which he suggests feelings about the cycle of all human living, the prose sketch is very limited. Its tone is similar to the poem, but the perceiving consciousness is that of a considerably younger person. (Sometimes, because the sketch has been printed as preface to *A Death in the Family*, it has been mistakenly assumed to be part of the novel.) "Knoxville" is the evocation of remembered summer evenings which Agee experienced in childhood. Through the sketch there is a movement back toward all summer evenings and then a concentration on an almost static single evening. What Agee caught was a "contemporaneous atmosphere" which permeated the experiencing of those evenings.

The remembered mood is suggested by a subtle combination of prose rhythm and metaphor, along with what at times appears to be almost straight description; and the juxtaposition of the following sentences is illustrative of Agee's method: "The hoses were attached at spiggots that stood out of the brick foundations of houses. The nozzles were variously set but usually so there was a long sweet stream of spray, the nozzle wet in the hand, the water trickling the right forearm and the peeled-back cuff, the water whishing out of a long loose and low-curved cone, and so gentle a sound."[24] The first sentence, because it is matter of fact, is short and succinct. The second one is more elaborate because the thought behind it is more complex. The beauty of the water hoses is conveyed by rhythmic constructions and the barest hint of metaphor. The alliterative *s* ("sweet stream of spray") is found near the beginning of the second sentence, and this unity helps to suggest the unity of the experience. In the same way, the words "the water whishing out of a long loose and low-curved cone" also suggest the motion of the water which was so enjoyed. And that enjoyment was something in which all of the senses participated. The flow of water brought with it "so gentle a sound"; it was a "sweet stream." Somehow, the "tenderness" of the experience suggested that the water must also taste good.

The sketch also is unified by the various sounds heard in the night. The hoses, the locusts, and even the streetcars make sounds, all of which blend into a unity. But each retains its distinctness. In a way, hearing all the sounds of the evening was like hearing a symphony. And thus, Agee's representation of that evening also possesses musical qualities. Of the sound of the hoses, he says, in part: "First an insane noise of violence in the nozzle, then the still irregular sound of adjustment, then the soothing into steadiness and a pitch as accurately tuned to the size and style of stream as any violin. . . ." In the description of the water hoses, Agee employs several methods to suggest the quality of the evening, and the rhythm of the prose strengthens the representation of the evening. When harsh, irregular, and violent sounds are suggested, the syntax is irregular; and, as the stream is smoothed "into steadiness" and becomes "as accurately tuned as a violin," the sentence pattern becomes smoother. Even the houses suggested a harmony. The speaker remembers how the "gracefully fretted houses" "corresponded" and how "the yards ran into each other with only now and then a low hedge that wasn't doing very well."

An important characteristic of this prose (and possibly the first extended presentation of it in all of Agee's work) is the idea underlying the remembrance: he suggests that a sure aesthetic sense was present when the beauty of all those sounds was heard; but the awareness was not conscious. His point is, of course, that there is no borderline between "art" and life, but the beauty of life is seldom mediated except by artists. Only an artist thinks to say the hoses "were set much alike, in a compromise between distance and tenderness . . . and [that there was] quite surely a sense of art behind this compromise." As the evening is remembered, the fact that a hose made a "snorting" noise, or that some man "decorated" the evening with his nozzle, stands as an isolated event singled out from the unity of the evening. If any of the sense impressions of the evening were stopped, there would have been a noticeable gap as if some creature had been removed from existence—and the world "left empty, like God by the sparrow's fall." But the sensing of the evening was not something reflected upon at that moment. Each man hosed his lawn, "happy and peaceful, tasting the mean goodness of their living like the last of their supper in their mouths. . . ." The appreciation of those evenings was not something verbal or even mental. Rather, it was sensed with the whole being; and Agee's prose evokes the unity of that impression.

Another work, neither an experiment nor an attempt to evoke personal memories, is the "Lines Suggested by a Tennessee Song." Of an indeterminate date, this poem illustrates Agee's continued use of material based on memories of his Tennessee origins. This nativity ballad derives from folk material:

> Mary was the sweetest gal
> a hundred mile around.
> Lively and kind and good to see
> as ever might be found.[25]

The poem is a simple retelling of the story of Mary, her wedding to Joseph, the annunciation, and the birth "in a cold black barn":

> She could a had the best hotel,
> doctors, a fine gold ring,
> name in the papers and winter-flowers,
>   for He was King.

This song is a quiet, understated accomplishment.

VI *Documentation of Actuality*

While Agee did write, at least a little, about memories of Tennessee during the 1930s, over a decade passed before he devoted a significant amount of energy to such remembrances. His writing for *Fortune*, then *Let Us Now Praise Famous Men*, and film criticism occupied most of the decade. Two essays, written for *Fortune*, are significant examples of his analytical journalism; but they also demonstrate how his interest in honoring actuality was being refined toward the precision of the non-fictional method used in *Let Us Now Praise Famous Men*.

The first of these essays "Six Days at Sea" involves a method which Agee knew might be expanded. In his "Plans for Work," he listed as a possible project "an account and analysis of a cruise: 'high'-class people," which would have as its technique the procedure "developed part way in *Havana Cruise*." "Six Days at Sea" is that account in which Agee reports the boredom and anxiety of the cruise passengers who often attempt to act as though they are having a good time. How they simultaneously reveal fears and social background is fascinating. The tone emerges from a realization that the passengers cannot have a good time because they have lost any ability to accept life without its accompanying complicated norms. In their desires to do the right thing at the right time, they forget still other things. In being concerned about what costume to wear, they forgot how to enjoy the water. The title of the article is ironic, and implies the voyage was boring. Agee suggests that the veneer of conventionality must be stripped away to record the reality of how the passengers felt. Related to this essay is the short story "Before God and This Company," which describes a New York party, for emptiness is found both in lives of the pseudosophisticated and in those who buy cruise tickets.

The closing section of Agee's account of a "pleasure" cruise is representative of a poetic prose he sometimes produced for *Fortune* and suggests the appearance of New York to the returning reporter:

The city stood apparelled in the sober purple and silver of supreme glory, no foal of nature, nor intention of man, but one sublime organism, singular and uncreated; and it stretched upward from its stone roots in the water as if it were lifted on a dream. Nor yet was it soft nor immaterial. Every window, every wheatlike stone, was distinct on the eye as a razor and serenely, lost, somnabulists the buildings turned one past another upon the bias of the ship's ghostly movement, not unlike those apostolic figures who parade with the clock's noon in Strasbourg.[26]

This technique, which includes the subjective, was refined within *Famous Men*, but another step along the way to it was an article about Brooklyn that was rejected by *Fortune*. Father Flye once wrote Agee to encourage him in plans to portray "the spirit and personality of a city";[27] and Agee's essay "Southeast of the Island: Travel Notes," published posthumously, is just that—an approach to the particular phenomenon of Brooklyn. In a minor key, this essay serves to balance the harsh facts recorded about the South in *Famous Men*, for the cramped and crowded conditions of middle-class or lower-class life in Brooklyn are no more appealing to the young writer than the constrictions of sharecropping. The "travel notes" on Brooklyn are harsh, but each evidence of caustic reaction to what was observed is balanced by a tempered insight about a vast city which is but a satellite of Manhattan. Agee's eye seeks out details perhaps unnoticed by others; the facts are there, he seems to imply; but they have not been noticed. Agee saw beauty and pathos in the stuff of ordinary life, and he sought to give some idea of the effect on persons of the flat and monotonous landscape of Brooklyn. To look at an ordinary street in Brooklyn and to find ways to reveal what was seen became fundamental to Agee's developing aesthetic. His sketch seeks out the truth of the commonplace, which has an importance and a fascination which those who surround it might not notice.

Agee's friend Walker Evans was photographing scenes in New York at this time, and one of Evans' favorite subjects was subway passengers. Eventually, Agee wrote an introduction for those photographs. To catch the diversity of persons seen in a large city is at the heart of his essay about Brooklyn: "Watching them in the trolleys, or along the inexhaustible reduplications of the streets of their small tradings and their sleep, one comes to notice, even in the most urgently poor, a curious quality in the eyes and at the corners of the mouths, relative to what is seen on Manhattan Island: a kind of drugged softness or narcotic relaxation."[28] By reporting the actuality much is implied. Agee documents lives made possible because of certain surroundings and material goods, lives for which an escape from Manhattan is essential. There can be no Manhattan without Brooklyn, and the reverse as well; to escape is only a relative thing, and all escapes "bestow their own peculiar forms of bondage."

This essay is deliberately organized to emphasize that its subject matter is immense. Agee's procedure is to begin over and over, and then to begin again. After pages have been used to suggest the complexity of the many districts, and the visits which have been made to them begin to give the sense of these various neighborhoods, Agee appends what he labels "A social note." There he provides details about his own experience. Toward the end of the article still more images seem, at first, disconnected; but the net effect is to suggest that a camera has been used discriminately on the streets of Brooklyn. The concluding paragraphs are pictures of the Brooklyn zoo, not a particularly pleasant place, but exactly the right image to suggest what, in fact, the city is.

CHAPTER 4

The Tenant Book

I Unimagined Reality

WHEN Agee learned that he and Walker Evans were to prepare an article for *Fortune* about Southern tenant farming, he was enthusiastic with the prospect because it would provide substantial material for which he could utilize his theories about nonfiction. He certainly sensed that his way of approaching such a subject would be less than mild-mannered and more than straightforward. He and Evans were assigned to travel into the Deep South to obtain material for a magazine article which was to have as subject matter "an average white family of tenant farmers."

The article was written, but never reached publication. Agee had doubts about being able to write adequately about tenant farming before he ever made the trip. In a letter to Father Flye, he said he felt the Alabama project was the "best break" he had received since being on *Fortune*; but he simultaneously expressed "considerable doubts" about his ability to bring it off as it seemed "in theory" to call for expression.[1] His doubts were made certain after some eight weeks in Alabama, for he rather explicitly later wrote that "The trip was very hard, . . . one of the best things I've ever had happen . . . . Writing what we found is a different matter. Impossible in any form and length Fortune can use. . . ."[2]

Some of his findings became *Let Us Now Praise Famous Men*, published five years later, Agee's most controversial, unusual, innovative, and careful accomplishment—and certainly his masterwork. In an excellent but somewhat contradictory notebook comment about the content of his text, Agee indicated that at the book's "centre" was to be found each of the following: particular moments actually experienced; himself (and his consciousness); and the persons who were the ostensible subject matter.[3] In 1937, he speculated

how he would handle that diverse material: "Any given body of experience is sufficiently complex and ramified to require . . . more
than one mode of reproduction: it is likely that this one will require
many, including some that will extend writing and observing
methods . . . the job is perhaps chiefly a skeptical study of the
nature of reality and of the false nature of re-creation and of communication."[4] In other words, many stylistic methods were
necessary.

But, when the book was published, no one seemed particularly
interested in an experiment in communication; and its reception
and sales combined to make *Famous Men* one of the most spectacular publishing failures of 1941. America, about to enter the war,
had little interest in what appeared to be still another book about
social problems like so many of the preceding decade. There were
notable exceptions to the cool or hostile reviews.[5] But many
reviewers were either hesitant to commit themselves about the
seemingly strange format of the book, or they castigated Agee, who,
they felt, was too much present within a book supposedly about cotton farmers. A typical comment was: "Agee's bad manners, ex-
hibitionism, and verbosity are a sort of author's curse at his own
foredoomed failure to convey all that he feels."[6] Another reviewer
suggested not only that Agee was too much present within the book
but that he "does a good deal to antagonize his reader. There are
too many tongues, too many attitudes, too many awarenesses on the
subjective side (perhaps defenses would be more precise); even the
sincerity is too much, too prostrate."[7] Little time was spent by initial reviewers in an attempt to understand why Agee felt his unusual procedures were necessary.

Despite the initial awkward reception of *Famous Men*, it slowly
gained a reputation in the years following publication. Among the
small group of readers who admired Agee's work, the book became
respected; and, even before Agee's death in 1955, a first edition of
Famous Men was a collector's item. By 1960, when it was repub-
lished, Erik Wensberg could comment: "It begins to appear that we
are present at the court's reversal and *Let Us Now Praise Famous
Men* is to be widely acknowledged as a great book. . . ."[8] Now it is
acknowledged a classic documentary. Subsequent critical studies

and approaches illustrate the complexity of its unusual text and confirm that Agee's text is simultaneously an experiment in communication and an accurate picture of what he beheld.

Ohlin uses Agee's phrase, "an effort in human actuality," to support his analysis; and he argues that the text is "carefully structured
[and] its final effect depends on the design of the whole." He insists
that "the *only* way to see Agee's work is not as a book about
'sharecropping' but as a book about the writing of a book about
'sharecropping,' and this, in turn, means that what the reader is experiencing is not the ordinary fictionalized (or pseudo-fictionalized)
account of reality but the writer's performance of an action or
gesture in words as a response to an *actual* human situation."[9] That
performance is carefully ordered; Agee spent many years with the
composition; and his careful ordering of language demands detailed
examination. In contrast to Ohlin's study, Kenneth Seib's provides
only a short section on *Famous Men*, and for all practical purposes
he ignores Agee's technique and, unfortunately, concludes that the
book represents a failure of form.[10]   Other approaches to the text
emphasize important facets of this multidimensional work. In
studies by Alfred Barson and J. Douglas Perry, Jr., many valuable
insights are provided: Barson traces the development of Agee's artistic consciousness, but pays little attention to Agee's reaction to his
milieu; and Perry demonstrates that Agee's writing is related to the
American Romantic tradition. William Stott's book *Documentary
Expression and Thirties America* demonstrates how Agee's text goes
beyond any other "documentary" of the period.[11]

Agee's text both is and is not a "literary" work. His approaches to
reporting the *un*imagined had been in a process of gestation for
years preceding the trip to Alabama. A total experience, from
biography to the manner in which the book was set into type, ultimately became important to this text's composition. Agee's
attempt to wrestle with myriads of inaccuracies and distortions is
the core of the work. However, a fundamental assumption which
undergirds the text—ironically a work of "Art," despite Agee's
belabored distinctions that it is not—is that any attempt to provide
an accurate record of what he observed was doomed from the start.
For this reason, Agee insists on making his reader aware of the complexity of his goals. Within his text, Agee insists that he wanted to
provide an account "without either dissection into science, or diges-

tion into art, but with the whole of consciousness."[12]

A basic notion which had to be communicated was that distinct persons were apprehended within a unique texture. Each was "a human being, not like any other human being so much as he is like himself" (232). Because each was respected as distinct and "holy," the dignity of the human person is Agee's basic motif; his language and the obvious external use of religious forms support this fact. But, while trying to adhere to particularities, Agee knew that he had been affected by what was experienced. And he believed that his reactions were finally just as important as what had caused the reactions. *Famous Men*'s aesthetic, therefore, focuses attention on details as remembered, but often as modified by reflection. The writer's presence provides knowledge of the limitations of consciousness; but, since such knowledge is part of any accurately recorded experience, Agee's reactions are included.

The text is split between problems which faced Agee as he tried to write and his doubts about the morality of prying into the tenants' lives. The book proper begins: "It seems to me curious, not to say obscene and thoroughly terrifying, that it could occur to an association of human beings drawn together through need and chance for profit into a company, an organ of journalism, to pry intimately into the lives of an undefended and appallingly damaged group of human beings. . ." (7). What Agee experienced cannot be adequately communicated; he even says that, if it were possible, there would be "no writing at all" (13). Yet remembering that Beethoven once said, "He who understands my music can never know unhappiness again," Agee indicates that he must state the same of his perception; his qualification is that "performance . . . is another matter" (16).

Material for *Famous Men* was gathered by living with one family, the Gudgers, for a period of about one month; but close ties were also developed with two other families. Agee hoped that through such familiarity representative ideas could be gained about tenant farming in general. The text as a whole finally concerns itself not only with sharecroppers, or even with workers of the United States, but with all who live in the world.[13] In 1938, as he was preparing the manuscript, Agee wrote Father Flye to explain that he was faced with the problems of the subject matter "intensifying" itself. "The whole problem and nature of existence"[14] was present within his questioning mind. Therefore, while the text is a picture of his unique remembrance as he devises procedures appropriate for retelling, it also is a commentary about particular lives and about the fragility of man's existence. Many of the more meditative parts of the book suggest no writer more than Henry David Thoreau.

Agee's ornate structure suggests disunity, but it can as certainly be demonstrated that the text is carefully organized so that the reader will experience various kinds of reality—if he has the patience to be attentive—and to put up with the presence of the angry consciousness of James Agee.[15]

II   Levels of Communication

Famous Men functions like poetry even though Agee insists that a work of art was not intended. Living with the Gudger family had been a rich emotional experience; and, because Agee was inextricably involved with those about whom he wrote, his manner of presentation became lyrical. Personal emotion is basic to the text even when he writes about a very plain object or atmosphere. Agee wrote such "objects and atmospheres have a sufficient intrinsic beauty and stature that it might be well if the describer became more rather than less shameless," but immediately following this remark he notes that Jean Cocteau had remarked of Picasso that "the subject matter is merely the excuse for the painting, and . . . Picasso does away with the excuse" (239). Such a statement admits the importance of the writer's presence even when an object is presented for its own sake, such as all the contents of a particular bedroom drawer. Agee wants his reader to feel as close as possible to the living situation.

For this reason, the aural or musical quality of the text is fundamental. In the preamble Agee suggests that the text might be read aloud (he read the book aloud to friends as he wrote it); and he indicates that he is striving for a new literary form which would be analogous to music.[16] Ultimately, the form he developed relies upon several techniques which flow into one another. Particular kinds of experiences are emphasized within different units; and, because of the complexity of the variegated experience, several techniques were necessary. Agee knew readers might be surprised by his procedures: "The whole job may well seem messy to you. But a part of my point is that experience offers itself in richness and variety and in many more terms than one and that it may therefore be wise to record it no less variously" (244-45). Each variety of writing represents a facet of Agee's attempt to communicate the truth of unimagined reality. First, he wrote about "realities" that he himself had experienced. Second, he wrote about actual persons and events, and he did not gather material for a composite picture using bits of many lives and imagination. Third, because he realized millions face the same problems as those with whom he had lived, he had to communicate still another type of reality.

Agee himself, in the essay "On the Porch," a part of the book written early, spoke of approaching his technical problems "from four planes."[17] The first three of these modes of awareness correspond, in principle, with the aspects of the subject matter just noted: personal experience, knowledge of individuals and events, and generalization. (Agee's notebook entry about the many "centres" of the text also corroborates his systematic procedure.) The fourth plane (paragraph five below), is self-explanatory. Agee's suggestion of categories follows:

Very roughly I know that to get my own sort of truth out of the experience I must handle it from four planes:

That of recall; of reception, contemplation, *in medias res,* for which I have set up this silence under darkness on this front porch as a sort of forestage to which from time to time the action may have occasion to return.

'As it happened': the straight narrative at the prow as from the first to last day it cut unknown water.

By recall and memory from the present: which is a part of the experience: and this includes imagination, which in the other planes I swear myself against.

As I try to write it: problems of recording; which, too, are an organic part of the experience as a whole.

These are, obviously, in strong conflict. So is any piece of human experience. So, then, inevitably, is any even partially accurate attempt to give any experience as a whole. (243)

This outline provides a base upon which to build an analysis of the text, but it is, however, a highly qualified and unsystematic statement in which Agee adds qualification to qualification. Even his punctuation is confusing. The first and most important word in the initial group of phrases is "recall." After that introductory word, a semicolon appears, which indicates at least a partial termination of thought; the phrases which follow however qualify the word "recall." A colon would be appropriate since the following phrases clarify—"reception, contemplation, *in medias res.*"

Agee states that the early essay "On the Porch" belongs to his first category. Exmination shows that his concern in "On the Porch" is to write in the present about past events, emphasizing how he personally had undergone an experience. Since his writer's consciousness is central, "reception and contemplation" therefore are used in a special sense on the first plane; and they are concerned with the way in which Agee personally received what was later recalled. The three sections of "On the Porch" have a dual purpose: Agee records most importantly how he felt as he was lying on a Chevrolet cushion late one summer night on the front porch of George Gudger's house; but he also elaborates some of his technical problems. The initial section of "On the Porch" consists of but three pages which convey the intense quietness felt as silence enfolded the house while the Gudger family was "sunken not singularly but companionate . . . into a region prior to the youngest quaverings of creation" (21). As Agee recalls his mental state that night, the animals, the fields, and the sky all contributed to a feeling of harmony; and he remembers how his whole body sensed these interrelationships. His intense awareness is the prime fact communicated.

The second plane—"as it happened"—has a general correspondence with the need for communication of facts about individuals and particular things. The second plane of writing is well illustrated with "Second Introit," which deals, in fact, with Agee's second coming to the home of the Gudgers. On this plane, the writer gives his reader a sense of immediacy about events. Personal reactions and imaginative additions flowing from the experience are held to a minimum, for his fundamental aim is to report in significant detail items which contributed to an experience: physical objects, sensations, gesture, emotion. What takes place in "Second Introit" is simple, though it takes eleven pages to relate. Agee's car becomes stuck in the muddied road; he returns to the Gudger's, has a late evening meal, and retires. By relating what "happened" and by emphasizing particularities, Agee implies wider spans of reference. For example, in describing Annie Mae's posture, he suggests much about her personality; yet he is careful when employing this plane to emphasize what did happen: "After a few moments, during which I hear her breathing and a weary shuffling of her heels, she comes out barefooted carrying the lamp, frankly and profoundly sleepy as a child . . . she sits a little away from table out of courtesy . . ." (413). Each gesture and object observed is important. Not so important are reactions. The precision of the reporting allows the reader to draw conclusions.

Within the third plane—"recall and memory from the present"—Agee's awareness is extended away from the particulars with which he came into contact, and he may include generalizations about all who lead similar lives to those he observed. This plane is the only one upon which Agee felt "imagination" should be included, and here he is furthest removed from what he experienced in Alabama. "Recall," when used in reference to the third plane, has a totally different meaning from the same word employed in reference to the first plane: on the first, Agee's interest is to show his feelings when he underwent an experience; on the third plane, the primary design is to write of a total experience as recalled and modified by the imagination.[18] The fourth plane—"problems of recording"—is reflected throughout the text both in explicit statements, such as in the midpart of "On the Porch," and through the diverse approaches which implicitly suggest technical difficulties.

The third basic plane, "recall and memory from the present," informs the "Education" chapter in which Agee built upon what he had observed in Alabama. Pointing out that the section is "deductive," he often goes to great lengths to show that what he writes is inspired by fact but is partially constructed from imagination and extended beyond the education of just a few tenant farmers. This bloc is an indictment of all education. The monologue which opens the section reveals Agee's rage: "IN EVERY CHILD who is born, under no matter what circumstances, and of no matter what parents, the potentiality of the human race is born again: . . . we are too near one of the deepest intersections of pity, terror, doubt and guilt; and I feel that I can say only, that 'education' . . . does not seem to me to be all, or even anything, that it might be . . ." (289–90). The separate planes are not absolutely divisible, but frequently a single section is written with concentration on a single plane.

The concentration on a single plane can especially be recognized by a contrast of chapters, such as "Shelter" and "Work." The former is basically written from the second plane, "as it happened," and stands as a record of what Agee beheld. The latter, which includes generalizations, could apply to many tenants. As in the chapter on education, the writer recedes from view; for Agee's concern in "Shelter" is to give an image of particular families' homes and to describe things as he found them. Elaboration of emotion, although important, is held to a minimum. When writing in such a way, Agee is one remove from the thing about which he writes. "Work," more indirect, is based on information gathered from Bud Woods and others; and Agee's concern is to describe the reiterative qualities of common labor and how such work affects the human consciousness. His description applies to any person faced with similar work.

The arrangement of the text in *Famous Men* also indicates that different planes were consciously employed. The prose is divided into three parts. Part One, "A Country Letter," begins "*in medias res*" as Agee contemplates a burning coal-oil lamp; it reconstructs a state of mind as recalled. Agee wants his reader to see the bias of the writer. Throughout "A Country Letter," however, a movement exists from such specific details toward plane three, or generalization. Part One utilizes all three planes of writing and shows a definite movement from the first, Agee's own experience, toward the third plane, which includes imagination. Part Two includes the chapters about money, shelter, clothing, education, and work; and some sections of this part of the text rely heavily upon a retelling "as it happened." But the emphasis remains upon the reality implied by the remembrance of these: plane three.

"Some Findings and Comments" is the title given to Part Two in which Agee wants mostly to give information. Part Three, "Inductions," emphasizes the second plane, or retelling how things happened. Agee feels his readers are finally ready to draw conclusions. Yet here, too, the use of the imagination and generalization often appear; and the fourth plane, "problems of recording," is significant. When Agee was given a room to sleep in, he retells how he perceived it in this way: "The furniture stood, where I have begun to see, sober and naked to me in the solemn light, and seemed as might the furnishing of a box-car, a barn. This barn and box-car resemblance I use, it occurred to me then and since, as an indication of the bonelike plainness and as if fragility of the place; but I would not mislead or miscolor: this was a room of a human house, of a sort stood up by the hundreds of thousands . . ." (420–21). Although Agee consciously developed procedures for relating the diversity of his experiences, his presence remains fundamental; for his involvement is ultimately what brings unity to the book.

III   *The Encompassing Rhythm*

Agee's involvement is fundamental, and his text is carefully arranged to provide many kinds of information. That arrangement is so unusual, however, that some readers feel it fragmentary.[19] An overview of the book's many parts demonstrates how each functions. Some sections are a record of Agee's relationship to particular persons and documentation that he could not convey all that that relationship meant. Other parts are concerned with wider meaning providing an image of a way of life. Such disparate concerns are woven together through Agee's presence and through recurring motifs, and the resulting text provides much more than previous documentaries had even attempted.

Two quotations which precede the text serve as constantly recurring themes "in the sonata form" (xviii and xix). A speech of Lear's is first: "Expose thyself to feel what wretches feel"; and such empathy is encouraged through later emphasis on data about food, clothing, and shelter. Agee states "What an insult it is to those who must spend their lives eating [such food]: I shall eat for a few weeks what a million people spend their lives eating, and feel that whatever discomfort it brings me is little enough and willingly taken on, in the scale of all it could take to even us up" (417).

The familiar "Workers of the world, unite . . ." serves as the second epigraph, and it is brought to mind especially in the "Education" and "Money" chapters. Agee does not imply that radical changes can be made in these lives; but, while he does not propose answers to such complex social problems, he insists that the tenant farmers are "like revolutionists who must fight fire and iron and poison gas with barrel staves and with bare hands: except that they lack even the idea of revolution" (313). Because he does not

attempt to suggest "solutions," his primary effort is placed on
demonstrating the dignity of persons he knew. Just as with the
photographs of Evans, the purpose is to chronicle a way of life, not
to suggest how to change it.

How best to accomplish the task of recording was a problem for
which Agee lacked a complete answer. Because of his doubts about
procedure, he felt the book needed not only a preface and an
eleven-page preamble but also an additional twenty pages devoted
to a discussion of technical problems within the meditative "On the
Porch." Placed so that the reader sees what methods are used, that
discussion clarifies the technical procedure. Essentially Agee's point
is this: conveying as closely as possible a particular thing should
have a value in itself. Realizing the value of things undigested by
"art," he hopes that he can represent the "chain of truths" which
"did actually weave itself and run through" a few weeks in
Alabama (240).

Each part of the book is an attempt "to reproduce and analyze
the actual." Each major section echoes one or both of the two
recurring themes: "Feel . . . what wretches feel"; and "Workers
. . . Unite." Before Book Two begins (Book One is composed of
Evans' photographs) Agee includes several "Preliminaries." These
include the preface, the epigraphs which suggest recurring themes,
a quotation from a child's geography book, and a list of "Persons
and Places." The last item indicates Agee's feelings about his
relationship to his subject. He and Evans are the final persons
listed, and they are described as "a spy, traveling as a journalist"
and as "a counterspy, traveling as a photographer" (xxii).

After "Preliminaries," Book Two, the text, begins with three
short unrelated incidents: two encounters with Negroes, and a
chance meeting of three persons at a lonely farmhouse. These
narrative sections are written "as it happened," but they bear no
direct relationship to more specific reports about families Agee
knew. Because these narratives demonstrate the general state of the
South during the summer of 1936, they serve to support other sections by giving a semblance of the atmosphere under which Agee
and Evans lived and worked for many weeks. One idea is common
to all three incidents: a feeling of embarrassment about intrusion.
In the preamble, Agee emphasizes his doubt about his right to pry;
and this doubt remains a basic ingredient in all that follows.

"Late Sunday Morning" relates how Agee and Evans were escorted by a landowner to a farm where they, regrettably, interrupted a group of Negroes who were forced to sing for them. "At the Forks," describes a meeting with three "clients of rehabilitation"—a young couple and a deranged old man; of them Agee says:

> They were of a kind not safely to be described in an account claiming to be unimaginative or trustworthy, for they had too much and too outlandish beauty not to be legendary.
> The young man's eyes had the opal lightings of dark oil and, though he was watching me in a way that relaxed me to cold weakness of ignobility, they fed too strongly inward to draw to a focus. (33)

Details of conversation and gesture constitute the remembered encounter, but Agee's confusion and embarrassment are central. Leaving, he "walked back the little distance to the car with [his] shoulders and the back of [his] neck more scalded-feeling than if the sun were on them" (42).

"Near A Church" recaptures first impressions of a country church which was "paralyzing" in its "classicism." As Agee and Evans wondered how to enter it, a Negro couple passed and walked some fifty yards before Agee decided to inquire where permission could be obtained. Running, he startled the couple, and their surprise and fear, along with his shame and embarrassment, are the essence of these pages. Each of these incidents reflects the general tenor of the South, and Agee's immense respect for others as well as his anger that people are abused by actions like his.

Following these incidents, but before "Part One" of the text begins, a single page "All Over Alabama . . . " is devoted to an evocation of the quietness that enfolds a typical Alabama night, a quietness which covers the South. Here the reader's awareness is extended out from one isolated farm as preparation is made for the following section, Part One, "A Country Letter."

In "A Country Letter," Agee speaks about individuals and particular families, but he meditates especially about the conditions which all tenant farmers face. This "Letter" comprises some sixty pages. Set late at night, much like "On the Porch," the letter is a partial reconstruction of a mental state as remembered. Because imagination plays an important role, however, the emphasis is upon approaching the remembrance from the third plane, "recall and memory from the present." Agee begins with a specific physical situation: he describes details of a lighted oil lamp. Soon, however, he moves from the concrete to the abstract and takes as his subject the loneliness each person must suffer: "Not one other on earth, nor in any dream, that can care so much what comes to them, so that even as they sit at the lamp and eat their supper, the joke they are laughing at could not be so funny to anyone else" (53). As the letter develops, thoughts move continually from abstract to concrete. Through the walls, Agee hears sounds of children rustling and the words of their mother, Annie Mae. Of those inside, his thoughts begin especially to center upon Emma, the sister of Annie Mae, who had visited the family for a few days when she was on her way to join her husband. Forced to marry an older man, Annie Mae's predicament is a symbol for the loneliness all suffer.

Details about the remembrance of one night's progression, combined with the description of the night's movement through dawn and the rising of the Gudgers, provide the balance of the letter. Specifics about the meal in the evening and bits of conversation are mixed with products of the imagination. One section imaginatively constructs dreams which those lying inside might have been at that very moment dreaming. And dreams are constructed which apply to all men. As dawn breaks and the rising of the Gudgers is described, Agee imagines the other two families beginning their day. The day's beginning and breakfast is described as a "ceremony," but

breakfast is too serious a meal for speaking; and it is difficult and revolting to eat heavily before one is awake . . .

and the breakfast ended, the houses are broken open like pods in the increase of the sun, and they are scattered on the wind of a day's work.

(*How was it we were caught?*) (90–91)

More pages are devoted to a detailed account of driving George Gudger to the sawmill where he works.

Glimpses given, Agee feels that it is necessary to meditate formally about the conditions of *all* who lead similar lives—to "screen off all mysteries of [his] comminglings" with these people in his attempt to see "the sorry and brutal infuriate yet beautiful structures of the living which is upon each of you daily: and this in the cleanest terms I can learn to specify: must mediate, must attempt to record, your warm weird human lives each in relation to its world" (99). But Agee's task is immensely difficult because the very nature of each human existence is called into question. He calls this section "Colon" and at one point says it is "all one colon," perhaps meaning his entire experiment with words. In this meditative ten-page "Curtain Speech," which ends Part One, Agee takes human existence and its mysteries as subject matter. He relies heavily upon plane three, imagination, to extend the oration outward from particulars.

"Part Two," entitled "Some Findings and Comments," consists of five chapters, as well as the second section of "On the Porch." Here Agee provides particular data. His opening section "Money" is "as extreme a précis" as possible and is, therefore, limited to straight factual reporting. Emotions and Agee's own response to facts play a small part in this account of the realities of "Money." The sparseness of verbiage emphasizes the bleakness of the economy. Minimum facts suffice: "Gudger—a family of six—lives on ten dollars a month rations money during four months of the year. He has lived on eight, and on six" (117).

The next sections, "Shelter" and "Clothing," fit together in subject matter and in mode of presentation, but the emphasis remains on specifics. "Shelter" is the most complex section of the book, and a separate outline of its organization is provided. The core of "Shelter" is devoted to a description of Gudger's house, less detailed accounts of other homes, and appended "Notes." "Shelter" occupies about one fifth of the text; and it is written, for the most part, from the second plane—"as it happened." Agee writes about the Gudger house as if the reader were present with him when he made a sacrilegious violation of the house. In midmorning all the Gudgers are gone: "No one is at home, in all this house, in all this land. It is a long while before their return. I shall move as they would trust me not to, and as I could not, were they here. I shall touch nothing but as I would touch the most delicate wounds, the most dedicated objects" (135).

The general structure, the façade, the "room beneath" the house, the hallway, and many of the objects that contribute to its individuality are described. Even the exact placement of furniture is given. That furniture, items on shelves, and the arrangement of these things into a unity are "beautiful." But Agee notes that to "those who own and create this 'beauty' [it] is . . . irrelevant and undiscernible." He hopes that, by providing detail, he will both communicate some of what he perceived and emphasize the dignity of those upon whom he has intruded. Implicitly, he condemns those who might laugh or snicker at the simple way of life described.

The "Clothing" chapter is handled similarly to "Shelter" with an emphasis on detail. Here, however, Agee lets his imagination play a minor role. He uses both the second and third planes. The chapter is based on many isolated observations. For instance, he lists Annie Mae's clothes, but realizes that she is keenly conscious of her dress, and therefore speaks of her as she might be dressed if she were to go into Cookstown on Saturday. Careful attention is given to detail as perceived. The feeling against the body of overalls, the color, the texture, and the change caused by age and use are minutely presented.

The "Work" chapter is less deductive. As the final part of Agee's findings, "Work" represents the crucial part of this section. In fact, the unused manuscript for the book includes a much more detailed opening of "Work." The published chapter is only an abbreviated version. Variant paragraphs are devoted to attempts to suggest the difficulty of writing about the stultifying qualities of reiterative labor.[20] Agee knew that the final part of Part Two should "be an image of the very essence of their lives: that is of the work they do" (319). His technical problem was to communicate the "plainness and iterativeness" of work and the incalculably immense damage done individuals. Since a tenant "family exists for work," some of the questions raised in "A Country Letter" are reemphasized: "How were we caught?" Interspersed with this imaginative account is "the most detailed, vivid, and carefully instructive exposition available in print of the planting, cultivation, and picking of cotton."[21]

Before Part Three begins, Agee provides an "Intermission" with "Conversation in the Lobby." Here appear his answers to "Questions Which Face American Writers Today," which had been sent to him by the *Partisan Review*, but his answers were not printed "on the grounds that no magazine is under obligation to print an attack on itself, and that [Agee] had not answered the questions" (350). Agee wants to let his reader see his bias and to demonstrate his conviction that no question is easily answered.

Part Three is labeled "Inductions." Before this section is begun, Psalm Forty-two is printed, traditionally the prayer at the foot of the altar before Mass. This part of the book deals with Agee's "first meetings," and his initial encounters with Fred Ricketts, Bud Woods, and with the Gudgers are given in detail. The psalm suggests that it is with the same amount of reverence as one approaches Mass that Agee enacts his first meeting with these people. At least ten pages, under the title "Reversion," deal with a trip Agee and Evans made to Birmingham and with their subsequent return.

Often throughout "Part Three" direct address is used. In this way, Agee reveals his thoughts but his inability to speak when he first met these families. The reenactment provides a sense of communion and Agee is able to clarify his own first thoughts. Thus, he confirms that Fred Ricketts was terribly insecure: Agee suggests now he begins to know why: ". . . and there you were, when I came out of the courthouse, . . . and we sat and talked; or rather, you did the talking, and the loudest laughing at your own hyperboles . . . and watching me with fear from behind the glittering of laughter in your eyes, a fear that was saying, 'o lord god please for once, just for once, don't let this man laugh at me up his sleeve, or do me any meanness or harm' . . ." (361).

Throughout Part Three, Agee combines techniques used in isolated parts of the text. "Inductions" is a remembrance of the first contact with these farmers, perhaps of the memories that remained most vivid. Agee's intent is to describe the event "as it happened," but also to suggest the texture of those events. By placing the inductions near the end of the book, the preceding sections, both particular and general facts, assist the reader to draw conclusions.

Six pages, entitled "Shady Grove, Alabama, July 1936," follow "Inductions." This is a description of a cemetery only loosely connected with what had preceded, since most of the section is a detailed account of what was seen at Shady Grove.[22] But what Agee has experienced by living with the Gudgers affects his perception: "On the graves of children there are still pretty pieces of glass and china . . . and of these I knew, when Louise told me how precious her china dogs were to her and her glass lace dish, where they would go if she were soon drawn down . . . ." (438). Two pages follow "Shady Grove," unconnected with other parts of the book, which are glimpses of tenant children, innocents doomed to lives like their parents.

Next, the title statement is printed. From the Book of Ecclesiasticus, chapter 44, Agee's emphasis is placed on the ninth verse: "And some there be which have no memorial; who perished, as though they had never been; and are become as though they had never been born; and their children after them" (445). "Notes and appendices" follow to demonstrate that the subject has not been adequately treated. The book closes with a return to the "porch" and to the quietness when Agee's perception of experience seemed clear. Writing, clearly communicating the experience, is another thing.

IV   Particular Uses of Language

To approach this account of tenant farming by classifying techniques or by describing it is helpful, but Agee intended for the effect of the prose to be, as a whole, experienced as one listens to a musical composition. All parts are designed to blend together into what he described as a continuum.[23] When *Famous Men* functions as a continuum, its many "centres," outlined in Agee's notebook entry, and his four levels of writing begin to merge. The individuals, the events, and the writer's consciousness of them blend.

For Agee, the camera was the "central instrument of our time," and his immense respect for photography basically stems from the fact that it is "incapable of recording anything but absolute dry truth" (11 and 234). With that realization, he admitted as he catalogued what he saw, that a camera might, at times, do a more accurate job. Consciousness and language, however, also have merits. A writer—if he relies upon them as a good photographer uses a camera and if he is supported by poetic imagination—can give a sense of an experience as seen with eye and mind, both at a particular time and as recalled. Such a continuum is often achieved in Agee's text, and the pages headed "*The room beneath the house*" are a concise example of how he combined description with his mental reactions. These pages consist of six paragraphs and a prose poem (147–49). One particular event is recaptured; but simultaneously Agee reveals his feelings and places the Gudger family in focus through a controlled use of his imagination. In "*The room beneath the house*" Agee meditates upon a particular plot of ground "which might have been field, pasture, forest, mere indiscriminate land: by chance: . . . and in a suddenness alien to those rhythms the land had known these hundred millions of years, lumber of other land was brought rattling in yellow wagonloads and caught up between hammers . . ." (147).

The construction and decay of all houses is recalled, but in the paragraphs which follow Agee concentrates on the immediate scene beheld. He provides a prose poem about "*each new dwelling squared by men on air.*" To complete this meditation, he imagines similar houses which he had observed at other times. His reconstruction of this one chance experience is presented through qualifications and details gathered elsewhere. Such a blending allows the total experience, which began with looking under one particular frame structure, to be carried through to the moment when the passage describing this event is included within the text. Agee's appreciation of such chance moments, in another place described as "as different as the difference between a conducted tour of a prison and the first hours there as a prisoner" (409), is of basic significance.

Often, when Agee reconstructs a remembered event, he pays attention to minute details; but a parallel effect is a verbosity which can be distracting or even seem like an evasion. Such concentration on detail is related to the intention, stated in the preface, that ultimately nothing "however trivial it may seem" would be omitted from a record which at first it was hoped would be "exhaustive" (xiv and xv). Such particularity is not an attempt to avoid making judgments about what had been seen.[24] Agee believed that if he could suggest "the cruel radiance" (11) of particulars, the reader would be able to make the necessary judgments. Agee's respect for his observations is crucial to what he attempts. He knows that some of his material may seem to place undue emphasis on one aspect. He has been accused of a "failure of moral realism" because he insisted that these tenants were divine.[25] But Agee was surely aware of their shortcomings, and he chose to emphasize his love and the beauty he saw in their crude existence rather than to document deficiency. His stylized uses of language emphasize his reverence for what he learned from these "simple," ordinary people.

Erik Wensberg suggests that an outline of *Famous Men* reads like
the program for a Protestant Church service.[26] Religious con-
notations are associated with Agee's frequent employment of forms
belonging to an earlier era, sometimes archaic in sound. Thus, a
tone of reverence is built into this stark report: "Gudger has no
home, no land, no mule; none of the more important farming im-
plements. He must get all these of his landlord" (115). Another
harshly realistic description makes careful use of the word "thus":
"[Mrs. Woods] . . . Her dress is made at home of thin pillow-slip
cotton, plain at the throat, cut deep for nursing. . . . She wears a
'slip' beneath this dress but the materials of both are so thin that her
dark sweated nipples are stuck to them and show through, and it is
at her nipples, mainly, that the men keep looking. It is thus also that
she is dressed on sundays" (285).

This effective way of saying, "These are the only clothes that this
woman had," emphasizes her dignity; and with such under-
statements Agee insists on the divinity of common farmers. Similarly, actions of everyday life are described as part of a semireligious
ceremony. Telling of his first meeting with the Gudgers, or of his
first night in their home, is an "introit." The movements of the
family at dawn, before and during breakfast, are of "no beauty less"
and in "just such silence and solitude" as when he knelt as a boy at
the altar at Mass when "the body and blood of Christ was created"
(89). Describing the house as it appeared against the horizon at
sunset, Agee notes that it stood "before the approach of darkness as
a boat and as a sacrament" (220). The reverent tone of "Colon [the]
Curtain Speech" is increased by the consistent use of words and
metaphors which have religious association. That section,
separating Parts One and Two of the text, includes many religious
forms.

Other important aspects of Agee's use of language may be
analyzed. Uses of dialect are fundamental, for often a sprinkling of
it reminds the reader of his ignorance of the culture which surrounds tenant life. A controlled use of rhythmical language is still
another device sustained, as is the careful use of symbol and
metaphor. Agee's stylized language is closely related to his presence
throughout, for he constantly reminds readers that what they know
is filtered through him as intermediary. That presence is a central
characteristic of *Famous Men*, and one early reviewer of the book

observed that its "real interest . . . is as a study of its author."[27] Agee knew that, as he wrote *Famous Men*, the "texture" of events which he experienced would remain inexplicable; but that inexplicability and his wonder are finally responsible for his language. Specialized uses of language were precipitated, therefore, by the mystery of what he had seen.

Kenneth Burke's observations about the ubiquity of rhetoric in human situations help to explain why Agee relied so heavily on rhetorical patterns when he saw particular persons within a divided human community. Rhetoric is present in all communicative situations; the more complex a situation becomes, however, the greater becomes the need for rhetorical patterns.[28] Because this text was written partly in disgust with a glib, somewhat accepted "documentary" style which tended to oversimplify, its language contains an undercurrent of rebellion which also contributes to its rhetorical form. Agee was sure that most documentary writers were not deeply enough involved. The more intensely personal insights are generally, and accordingly more difficult to verbalize, the more obvious are needs for a structured presentation.

Burke insists that events such as those described by Agee must remain mysteries, ultimately to be communicated only by means of "incantation." Only a suggestion of the complexity of felt emotion can be transmitted through language. Thus, as a situation is more intensely felt, the need arises for a comprehensive way to express feeling; but, as feeling increases, the difficulty of communicating does also. Some means for unification of feeling with expression, of identifying with what has been felt becomes necessary. Identification in its simplest terms is a deliberate device, as used for instance by a politician. Franklin Roosevelt said, "You are farmers: I am a farmer myself," but Agee ironically places Roosevelt's words at the beginning of his "précis" on "Money" to imply that identification is vastly more complicated when one becomes involved with others as he himself did in the writing of *Famous Men*.

Because Agee's impressions and imaginative wanderings are central, they are most comprehensively approached as poetry. The most obvious instance of this subjective language functioning simultaneously as a lyrical and highly patterned rhetorical structure is found in "Colon: Curtain Speech," the meditative speech about how any consciousness is formed from a complexity of sensations.

Written as an interior monologue, the prose of this speech is tightly
organized—at times, highly formal. Its rhythms are those of a pulpit
delivery; it has a predictability of sentence structure. Key words and
phrases tie the passage together with a recurring pitch and stress
pattern. The basic device employed to convey the number of items
impinging upon human consciousness, is, however, an extended use
of metaphor. At least five dominant images recur throughout the
passage: crucifixion, flower, prison, water, and star. This speech
about the mystery of existence is highly patterned, but, because of
the definiteness of its patterns, it is not representative of the whole
text.

A passage less obviously planned to function rhetorically is more
useful as a demonstration of how the text functions. "A Country
Letter" is such a section; also a meditation, it is basically an account
of Agee's recollection of only a few hours. Included in the idea of
any "Letter" is its personal form of communication; and Agee implies that, with the simplicity of a letter written from the "country,"
he presents this meditation. (He was fascinated for years with the
letter as a mode of communication.)[29] Agee knows his rhetorical
task is not so simple as writing a letter. His basic strategy combines
a relatively concise representation of many things, seen or imagined, with glimpses of reactions, while remembering the mood of a
single night. He wants to mirror the complexity of remembered interrelationships, but his reflections spring from the calm surface of
one particular night's experience.

The contents of the "Letter" are primarily the images of his mind
as he recalls the experience of the night's movement toward dawn.
As suggested earlier, one part of the letter imagines what those lying inside the house may have been dreaming; and these dreams
are constructed so they apply to all who are oppressed by poverty.
These thoughts pass through the filter of the writer's mind. He
dreamed the dreams; and he structures the retelling. "In what way
were we trapped? where, our mistake: what, where. . . . Where
lost that bright health of love. . . . How, how did all this sink so
swift away, like the grand august cloud who gathers . . ." (78). No
answers appear to these questions. Agee poetically suggests the
situation of all who must struggle against unsure economic circumstances. His dream expands to include the delusion and disappointments of human love, and the loss of life itself. He writes so

that readers will be drawn into the mystery of what he is saying, and the rhetorical pattern emphasizes the hopelessness and mystery of all such lives. To suggest how quickly all hopes are expired he uses metaphor: the expectations of these people are like a promising summer rain cloud which appears only to sink swiftly away.

"A Country Letter," illustrative of the immediacy of Agee's prose, recapitulates one evening; and the mood it suggests, especially in the beginning, is peacefulness. Implied is Agee's realization that the peace he experienced was largely because of his acceptance of an immediate situation. As he watched an oil lamp burn, he saw the sweating of the oil in the upper surface of the globe, and he knew that the sweating was not something to "understand nor try to deduce," but simply something to "like" (50). The implication is that the tenant farmers experienced similar moments. With "A Country Letter," Agee provides a way for his sophisticated readers to begin to experience what he did. Such recreation of experience is, as well, the purpose of the entire text.

V   *An Image of Life*

A fundamental accomplishment of Agee's *Let Us Now Praise Famous Men* is its image of tenant farming. True, the book is simultaneously the record of Agee's interaction of consciousness with the events which generated it, but it is such a record so that a true image of a way of life can be provided. *Famous Men* is primarily a record of persons who are both materially and spiritually impoverished; yet, ironically, while they are shrunken in potentiality, there remains a dignity about their lives, the result of an intricate conjunction of land and living.

Agee pictures lives which are heavily dependent upon the land. The inhabitants of rural Alabama are locked into an existence of degradation. The fact that his visit came during the most intense part of the Depression serves to emphasize the bleakness of their lives. The dominance of natural forces is central to his vision of a way of life, for this culture draws its sustenance from the land, as does the cotton for which the family appears to exist. The structure of the text makes it apparent that everything about these lives is built around labor. Cotton is the main crop, and the raising of it is the main function of these lives, a job "by which one stays alive and in which one's life is made a cheated ruin" (326). After the preparation of the land and the planting have been minutely described, paragraphs are devoted to a consideration of the lull before picking. This "terrible leisure" is one of the worst times for the farmer, for "the year's fate is quietly fought out between agencies over which he has no control" (334). Then the cotton's growth and the picking are described.

After the long-awaited first bale is ginned, the family returns to its home: "It is as if those who were drawn in full by the sun and their own effort and sucked dry at a metal heart were restored, were sown once more at large upon the slow breaths of their country, in the precisions of some mechanic and superhuman hand" (347). The implication is that these people are part of a natural, yet somehow also unnatural, cycle.

Agee constantly assures his reader that it is impossible to know a way of life or to evoke it with a verbal approximation. There is no "average white tenant family." But his love for these persons and his rage at their degradation drove him to sketch the "dignity of [their] actuality."[30] This text, what he once called a "dissonant prologue," provides an image of a way of life.

CHAPTER 5

The Film Criticism

I *The "Amateur" as Critic*

A GEE'S interest in film began at an early age. Father Flye recalls that when he and young Rufus returned from their tour of Europe during the summer of 1925, they had little more than set foot to shore before Agee wanted to see the films he had missed.[1] Early letters are sprinkled with references to moving pictures, and Agee's correspondence with Dwight Macdonald demonstrates how Agee already was interested in films, "especially from the director's point of view," while at Exeter.[2] At Harvard, this interest deepened; and he remained intrigued throughout the 1930s with the possibilities of the cinema when he wrote the experimental screen plays *Man's Fate* and *The House.* Thus Agee had developed an awareness of the potentiality of film for over a decade before he began writing criticism of the movies regularly.

The process of writing *Famous Men* as an exercise in analysis and his position as a *Time* magazine book reviewer also prepared him to make film observations. But early in the 1940s Agee would never have dreamed that so much of his energy was to go into critical writing. Earlier he had stated that he would not write "steadily" for money unless it was work he could "do and believe in for itself."[3] Little did he know that his position as book reviewer, which began in 1939, was a prelude to another decade of journalism. Much of his journalism work was accompanied by feelings of guilt about an inability to do his own work. Ironically, one of the early books he reviewed was Herbert Gorman's biography of Joyce; there he was reminded of the faithfulness required of the artist. Joyce's life seemed "almost a Bible of what a great artist, an ultimately honest man is, and is up against."[4] During these same months, Agee leveled criticism at his own record as artist; and he accused himself of being "frequently a bad artist, impure of heart, and an immoral man."[5] Barson asserts that "the effect of writing for his living instead of living for his writing [was to grip] him in a paradoxical and destructive malaise throughout the war years."[6] But such an assertion is true only if one considers the critical writing insignificant. Many agree his film criticism is among the best ever produced in America.

Agee took his journalistic writing seriously. Reviewing books and films consumed most of his energy for nine years, and to complicate matters he was often unable to write reviews hastily. Sometimes he indicated in *The Nation* that he needed a week, or more, before he could adequately review a film; and similar difficulties confronted him with other writing. Many who knew him remember how he would rewrite a review or a *Time* story innumerable times. Such single-mindedness dissipated energy; yet that same concentration made his film criticism valuable. He insisted upon looking at each film carefully; his criticism is subjective, and at the base of his comments stand his moral judgments. He insisted that he was an "amateur" in the sense of being an impartial observer. He maintained that any film reveals its culture, but often the persons who make a film are unable to perceive critically. In his initial column, he suggested that professional concern "with technique, with the box-office, with bad traditions, or simply with work, can blur, or alter the angle of . . . judgment." He refused to remove himself from his commentary, and he sought to avoid a simplistic view. In the opening column, he reveals this commitment and his awareness of the power of film to influence viewers.

In a pattern which was to continue through all the criticism now gathered in *Agee on Film*, he wrote, "I also urge that *Ravaged Earth*, which is made of Japanese atrocities, be withdrawn until . . . careful enough minds, . . . shall have determined whether or not there is any morally responsible means of turning it loose on the public."[7] Whether such documentary footage was technically good, or even accurate, is secondary; Agee's ethical judgment is the fundamental consideration. Similar judgments appear throughout columns in *The Nation* written over some seven years; and his comments about Elizabeth Taylor's acting (132) or about hangovers (184), which some critics maintained got in the way of his subject, are essential. His reactions, as an "amateur," are a combination of his sense of beauty and of the morally correct.

In notes for an introduction to Helen Levitt's *A Way of Seeing*, he once noted: "The mind and the spirit are constantly formed by, and as constantly form, the senses, and misuse or neglect the senses only at grave peril to every possibility of wisdom and well-being."[8] To Agee, a successful motion picture similarly had to honor mind and senses. The problem with many films, as they were mass-produced in the 1930s and 1940s, was that their makers failed to have an awareness of the effect on mind and spirit. Despite this failure, Agee usually perceived some good within the most ordinary of films.

To be a film critic during the 1940s was a challenge, and that Agee consistently found good things to say about mediocre films was a surprise to some. In this period before American audiences had ready access to European films, Hollywood functioned like a factory; and, compounding the problems of isolation and mass production, the war apparently encouraged film makers to rely upon cliché, and innumerable bad films were produced. Yet Agee continually saw possibilities for film as a medium through which a modern artist could both tap the realistic and make poetry. When his movie criticism was later collected, some reviewers complained of an apparent inconsistent aesthetic. But Agee's veneration of reality and honor for the individual unifies his enthusiasm, just as in all of his characteristic work.

His objections to many films produced during the 1940s in the factorylike conditions of Hollywood were objections to a form of entertainment (or art) which fell short of its potentiality. Stereotype ideas, predictable acting, cheap sets, and ignorance of the audience combined to dishonor the reality that many films purported to present. Fundamental to this criticism, and recognized by Ohlin as a basic ingredient, is Agee's "respect for human reality." Such respect "makes it the function of art to picture as accurately and honestly as possible the inherent beauty and immediacy of life."[9]

Agee's comments about Vittorio De Sica's *Shoeshine* reveal what he liked, but seldom found. *Shoeshine* caught not only the "emotional directness" of the "story of two street boys who are caught almost by accident into the corrective machinery of the state" (279) but also the spirit of that complexity. In working notes for his review, Agee noted that the makers of *Shoeshine* had "captured the dubious world of 'social' art and turned it over to the humanistic tradition. The characterizations in *Shoeshine* are not deep or brilliant, yet you get more clearly than any movie I have seen, a realization of the complexity of interplay between the individual and the system, and his place in it. Both are accused, neither are accused; both are forgiven, nothing is forgiven."[10]

In his criticism, and in his scripts as well, Agee did not have a sense of freedom essential for the artist. He was either dealing with "finished products" or materials adapted for the screen.[11] But these reviews do articulate Agee's views. He felt films should be made without a distorting artifice. More frequently than not, he was disappointed with the machinery responsible for much of modern movies, machinery which made it almost impossible for ordinary common sense—closely related to artistic sense—to survive.

II   "Comedy's Greatest Era"

Much of what Agee felt was wrong with movies is contrasted with what he sensed was right with the best from the silent era, a time when the visual image was predominant. His most sustained piece of criticism is an essay about silent comedies, films which possessed an honesty undistorted by any intermediary veneer—and films which made audiences laugh. Agee evokes essentially a mood of nostalgia about the silent era, and the style of "Comedy's Greatest Era" reflects his decision to build on personal response. Silent comedies were enjoyed because comedians knew how to suggest nuances without verbal assistance; and, with the introduction of sound, good comedy deteriorated. "When a modern comedian gets hit on the head, for example, the most he is apt to do is look sleepy. When a silent comedian got hit on the head he seldom let it go so flatly. . . . It was his business to be as funny as possible physically, without the help or hindrance of words" (3). To communicate his appreciation of such accomplishments Agee relied upon a style which suggested the filmic images. Since he knew that his readers would be persons who had not seen the films, or at least not recently, he provided in capsule fashion phrases about actors such as Harold Lloyd who "smiled a great deal and looked like the sort of eager young man who might have quit divinity school to hustle brushes," or Buster Keaton who "carried a face as still and sad as a daguerreotype."

His criteria for judging the success of silent comedy was laughter.

The essay begins with definitions of the "titter, the yowl, the belly-laugh and the boffo." Modern comedy clearly had come into an era of famine because most moviegoers only occasionally got beyond the yowl; and Agee's essay, which generated a lot of favorable mail, suggests that many thousands felt as he did. He emphasized that the best silent comedians were aware of what it means to be human. Chaplin, Agee suggested, created a figure in the tramp who was "as centrally representative of humanity, as many-sided and mysterious as Hamlet, and it seems unlikely that any dancer or actor can ever have excelled him in eloquence, variety or poignancy of motion" (9). Other comedians like Harry Langdon could, perhaps in a more limited way than Chaplin, produce a laugh which also revealed "subtle emotional and mental processes." In one scene, Langdon, "watching a brazen showgirl change her clothes . . . sat motionless, back to camera, and registered the whole lexicon of lost innocence, shock, disapproval and disgust, with the back of his neck" (13); and such mastery of detail fascinated Agee. The silent films he admits, were often shunned by "nice" people; "but millions of less pretentious people loved their sincerity and sweetness, their wild-animal innocence and glorious vitality. They could not put these feelings into words, but they flocked to the silents" (6). In contrast, in many films of the 1940s both individual talent and a respect for the audience seemed to have been lost. For this reason, Agee's criticism was often heavily concerned with the mistakes Hollywood incurred because it forgot that much could be revealed in little.

III   *"Hollywood Blindness"*

The American film industry had the techniques for capturing all aspects of reality, but what was often accomplished was barely lukewarm. In Agee's opinion, many American films were "sick unto death," because the possibilities for suggesting and recording reality were too frequently systematically ignored. To his mind, a blending of studio action, romantic characterizations, and documentary footage, as was the case with many "semi-documentaries" about the war, "chemically guaranteed the defeat of all possible reality" (67). Moreover, he felt the big studios consistently underrated their audiences; and he was disappointed that spectators were treated as fools because he knew that they were more perceptive than Hollywood assumed. Once he commented about a film which he theorized must have been designed with two endings: the ending of *The Curse of the Cat People*, as produced, must have slipped by the production office because it demanded more thought from an audience than ordinary box-office fare. Agee saw this film at a West Times Square theater; and the audience, one of the hardest imaginable to please, he noted, was satisfied. They did not feel they had been betrayed:

Masquerading as a routine case of Grade B horrors—and it does very well at that job—the picture is in fact a brave, sensitive, and admirable little psychological melodrama about a lonely six year old girl. . . . when the picture ended and it was clear beyond further suspense that anyone who had come to see a story about curses and were-cats should have stayed away, they clearly did not feel sold out; for an hour they had been captivated by the poetry and danger of childhood, and they showed it in their thorough applause. (85-86)

Hollywood usually gave audiences what it assumed they wanted. Thus, cliché and twistings of images often resulted in films which suggested nothing better than neurosis. Such inappropriateness was unsatisfactory. Even more disturbing was the fact that a bad film, like *Tender Comrade*, "an infinitely degraded and slickened *Little Women*" (90), was "likely to move, console, corroborate, and give eloquence to" much of America. Such commercialization of bad taste exemplified the distorted emphasis and vulgarity which made Agee ill at ease. For similar reasons he laughed at the distortions within the Esther Williams' film *Bathing Beauty*, which unnaturally swarmed "with bathing suits and their contents" (101). The dishonesty of such productions insulted audiences. Agee felt the same was true of Hollywood's insistence on contriving inappropriate sets while the world waited to be photographed.

An example of his objections to bad sets and improper locales is his reaction to *Dragon Seed*, an adaptation of the Pearl S. Buck novel and "an almost unimaginably bad movie." In it, California hillsides were terraced and dyed green for a proper effect; and, as if that were not bad enough, the dialogue was atrocious. Such talk as " 'the wind has brought the rain' instead of 'it's raining,' " made the picture more stilted. Characteristically, Agee hastened to qualify that "finding a diction proper to so-called simple folk is one of the most embarrassing . . . literary problems we have set ourselves" (109).

In Agee's opinion, film makers had no right to film a foreign culture of which they were ignorant. *The North Star* was an attempt to reflect the conduct of a small Russian village on the border during the opening days of the war, but both audience and imagined village were mistreated: for "every attempt to use a reality brings the romantic juice and the annihilation of any possible reality pouring from every gland" (57). To impose such false interpretation made things worse: "The result is one long orgy of meeching, sugaring, propitiation, which as a matter of fact, enlists, develops, and infallibly corrupts a good deal of intelligence, trust, courage, and disinterestedness." Sometimes, when realistic shots appeared in factory films, they remained isolated, never to gather any "cinematic momentum" (84). A concern with slickness, a finished product in which all parts have a nice surface like "cosmetics on a cadaver" (92), often defeated the good qualities in a film.

Agee insisted time after time that ordinary beauty is lost when falsely made to look pretty. For such reasons, he often argued that nonprofessional actors could do a better job of catching the immediacy of life than professionals. He was convinced that "art and actuality work on each other like live chemicals" (223), if a correct balance is maintained. But, within the framework of a factory film, actors often could not pretend to be revealing real persons. (When Agee's criticism was collected, his ideas about amateur actors were often attacked. But, as he himself emphasized, his preference is for a language of images which reveals the real. If "acting" detracted from reality, then it should be sacrificed.) The chief interest of a good film maker should be to reveal reality, and the Hollywood star-system often only obscured it.

IV   *Poetic Realism*

Given his objections, Agee's preference was for a blending of realism and poetry. Reality was to be honored in a way that its individual parts would manifest their beauty.[12] A successful film, therefore, was one which allowed natural beauty to shine. Agee admired the combat film *Desert Victory* because it stood as "a clean, simple demonstration that creative imagination is the only possible substitute for the plainest sort of good sense—and is, after all, mere-

ly an intensification of good sense to the point of incandescence"
(33). In that nonfiction film, images were respected for themselves;
and the honesty of the film became its unifying factor. A few years
later, writing about *San Pietro* directed by John Huston, Agee noted
a similar success: "close to the essence of the power of moving pictures is the fact that they can give you things to look at, clear of urg-
ing or comment, and so ordered that they are radiant with il-
limitable suggestions of meaning and mystery." Huston's use of
wordless children toward the end of that film was a "great passage
of war poetry" (164). In Agee's opinion, a successful film blended
reality with imagination; and, to him, André Malraux's *Man's Hope*
was such a success. He noted that commonly "movie and musical
form are closely related," while few films demonstrated awareness
of that relationship; but in *Man's Hope* all its parts blended
together—even the shots which suggested an "excess of energy,"
"letting things and movements into [the] frame which have nothing
to do with the central action . . . little things which brilliantly lock
men and their efforts and feelings into the exact real place and time
of day" (240).

Agee admired films which suggested the complexity of life itself.
His admiration for a blending of different images, combining the
expected and unexpected, is central to his admiration for Vigo's
Zero de Conduite. There the subjective and the objective, the fan-
tastic reality of the subconscious along with the conscious, blended
together. Agee believed that a film maker could appropriately combine several different methods as long as all of those methods were
attempts to divulge the truth.

Agee's defense of *The Miracle of Morgan's Creek* makes clear his
approval of Vigo's film. He noted a shiftiness of style; but he insisted, "if you accept that principle in Joyce or in Picasso, you will
examine with interest how brilliantly it can be applied in moving
pictures and how equally promising" (75). His fundamental
criterion for a successful film was freshness and vitality, a spirit
close to actual experience. Such freshness was accomplished in
Rossellini's *Open City* in which the performance of Anna Magnani
was near "the poetic-realistic root of attitude from which the grand
trunk of movies at their best would have to grow" (195).

It is clear why Agee disliked film imitations of imitations, for his
technical observations are closely related to the aesthetic he out-

lined in his call for poetic realism. A good director should honor his audience by making a film more than just a passive instrument. Agee knew that the effective use of the single shot, the judicious use of cutting, stop-shots, slow motion, and repetition contributed to the total effect. Properly used, such procedures could help a director to mirror reality. Similarly, the use of actual localities rather than contrived sets and the proper use of background music and color to support mood could contribute to the rhythm of a work.

A film which illustrated successful uses of technique blended with a respect for reality was *Farrebique*, which chronicled the lives of ordinary French farmers. Its director, George Rouquier, realized "that, scrupulously handled, the camera can do what nothing else in the world can do: . . . record unaltered reality." Agee's admiration of *Farrebique* is an indication of his guiding aesthetic, for the honesty of that documentary resulted in far more than documentation: "One could watch the people alone, indefinitely long, for the inference of his handling of them, to realize that moral clearness and probity are indispensable to work of this kind, and to realize with fuller contempt than ever before how consistently in our time so-called simple people, fictional and non-fictional are betrayed by artists and by audiences . . . " (297). Other critics charged that *Farrebique* was repetitious, and Agee agreed that indeed this was so—in exactly the same way as "the imitation and counterpoint and recurrence in a Mozart symphony are repetitious, and somewhat near as satisfying" (298).

V   *Moral Judgment*

Always implied, and sometimes categorically stated, is the moral stance which supports Agee's criticism. Agee repeatedly insisted that the motion picture possessed enormous power to reveal the depths of the human condition; and he was angry when such possibilities were ignored. Huston's *San Pietro* was a success because of its honesty: its footage was shot during combat; veteran soldiers were participants; the film was then developed in Washington; and, on his return to the States, Huston edited it. At the heart of what he accomplished was attention to the complexity and interaction of battle, its participants, the villages, and nature itself. The film possessed clarity and moral integrity because it grew out of something Huston and his crew respected.

Agee felt that no one had a right to make a film about something he did not understand, but the misunderstanding and its attendant errors were fascinating to him. He often saw the cinema as a revelation of culture; and he occasionally referred to films as collective dreams. Even a not particularly good picture revealed facets of the culture which generated it. Writing about *The Blue Dahlia*, he said it is "neatly stylized and synchronized, and as uninterested in moral excitement, as a good ballet; it knows its own weight and size perfectly and carries them gracefully and without self-importance." In its uninsistent way, the film "does carry a certain amount of social criticism," for it "crawls with American types; and their mannerisms and affectations, and their chief preoccupations . . ." (203). Agee wanted audiences to develop abilities to see such things, but the problem was that many viewers had never learned how to discriminate.

A film made and viewed in the proper spirit should suggest potentialities lost and the possibilities man has for gain. Such insights remain at the heart of Agee's desideratum. He once wrote, "The films I most eagerly look forward to will not be documentaries but works of pure fiction, played against and into, and in collaboration with unrehearsed and uninvented reality" (237). Such expectations account for Agee's admiration of Chaplin's *Monsieur Verdoux*, a film he regarded as a statement about man's loss of individualism. In order to provide a livelihood for his family, Verdoux was driven to extreme measures. To keep his family in isolation, Verdoux became a professional murderer who married and then killed rich women for their money. Such actions were necessary to survive at all in modern society; therefore, *Verdoux*, Agee suggested, was "a metaphor for the modern personality." To Agee, *Verdoux* was successful because, as in all of Chaplin's work, the best elements of primitive and civilized art were blended without weakening each other. *Verdoux* contained scenes of hilarious humor, but they were always enforced by seriousness. The film indicted modern civilization, but it did so by demonstrating how inextricably bound good and evil remain.

CHAPTER 6

Individualism

I

WHEN a single most representative motif is isolated from Agee's film criticism, that motif distills his arguments about falsification of reality and disrespect for persons—crimes for which bad film making should be indicted. The fact that film makers did not honor reality seemed symptomatic of a malady of the entire culture. Additional writing from the 1940s, some unpublished, indicates Agee's concern for individuals in what appeared to be a harsh and unloving world. He knew that "art and actuality" should "work on each other like live chemicals,"[1] but he feared that many of his contemporaries, not just film makers, had lost respect for the dignity of persons. World War II, climaxed by the use of the atomic bomb, made it difficult to maintain hope. Indeed, Agee once suggested that, after American civilization had disintegrated, one could deduce from its "nonfiction films alone" the reason for the collapse from the fact that so few "honored . . . others, or even themselves."[2]

As a writer, Agee never thought of his vocation in isolation from other responsibilities, and this dedication is illustrated by one of the seemingly incongruous parts of *Famous Men*, "Intermission in the Lobby." His inclusion of answers to a set of questions posed in 1939 by the *Partisan Review* emphasizes that he did not feel different private and public responsibilities. As culmination to a series about the interrelationships of vocation to society, the question was posed: "What do you think the responsibilities of writers in general are when and if war comes?" Agee's reply reflects his perplexity: "I am . . . confused between 'responsibilities' as a 'writer' and a 'human being'; which I would presume are identical . . . in other words, I consider myself to have been continuously at war for some years, and can imagine no form of armistice."³ This responsibility, exercised throughout his career, was especially apparent in the 1940s; for, just as he would not isolate himself from the personal problems of friends, he could not immerse himself in creative work and turn his back to the world. Father Flye once remarked that the idea of Agee as a starving writer ignoring the world for the sake of art was "unthinkable."⁴ Agee was attuned to the world and other people, and he saw little separation between being a good person and a good writer. For him the 1940s were especially difficult years in which to write with integrity.

Nevertheless, his personal and creative life during these years took a new and more productive shape. The period from late 1941 until he began to write filmscripts some seven years later unfortunately has been described as a period of wandering in the wilderness.⁵ It was, in fact, a period during which his married life was stabilized; and he began to do some of his best work. In 1944 Agee married Mia Fritsch, a researcher for *Fortune*; and the stability of their marriage, and later, the financial assistance which she provided, encouraged him to return to creative writing. However, as his family grew, much of his subsequent writing about and for movies was for financial reasons, for he would not rely upon others for support. No doubt, during the final years of his life Agee enjoyed being the "storyteller" for films.⁶

In the spring of 1946, the Agees bought a farm near Hillsdale, New York, described by Mrs. Agee as "absolutely nowhere, in the hills. The house . . . simple, even primitive. . . ." She remembers that Agee "was happiest in the country, but he [also] liked the stimulation of people in the city. He hated the commuting idea. It meant missing the advantages of both city and country life."⁷ The fact that they owned the farm, that he found pleasure working there, but that he simultaneously enjoyed the stimulation of the city is emblematic of his career during the latter part of his life: he knew that he needed discipline and peace to write, but he thrived on contact with others. And he pushed himself toward a maximum amount of involvement.

While Agee worked for *Time* and simultaneously wrote the film column for *The Nation*, he devoted almost all of his energy to those jobs. In typical *Time* manner, in brief essays seldom over two hundred words, he reviewed over one hundred books during the years

1939–1942; but he found it difficult to write book reviews. As has been observed earlier, "he couldn't develop a quick knack at judging."[8] He probably felt relieved when he was shifted to reviewing movies for *Time* and later when he was given more freedom as a special essay writer for the magazine. Some of those special articles reflect his developing thought during and immediately after the war years. For example, his essay about the atomic bomb illustrates his ability to write about a public event and to stress its relationship to the individual. Father Flye remembers that Agee was very much distressed on the day the bomb was dropped; he came to Flye's apartment to ask if he had heard the radio news; and, when Flye replied he had not, Agee insisted that he sit down.[9] His *Time* essay reflects in a style idiosyncratically his own his musings but stresses the importance of that horrible event for all mankind. Agee knew that all men were implicated:

> The promise of good and of evil bordered alike on the infinite—with this further, terrible split in the fact: that upon a people already so nearly drowned in materialism even in peacetime, the good uses of this power might easily bring disaster as prodigious as the evil. . . . When the bomb split open the universe and revealed the prospect of the infinitely extraordinary, it also revealed the oldest, simplest, commonest, most neglected and most important of facts: that each man is eternally and above all else responsible for his own soul, and in the terrible words of the Psalmist, that no man may deliver his brother, nor make agreement unto God for him.[10]

The bombing, done ostensibly for the good of many, stood as the extreme illustration of individual abnegation of responsibilities.

To act as an individual seemed especially difficult in a society which constantly generated tension between the individual act and actions done in the name of a group. In a 1945 letter, Agee stated that the "only thing much worth writing or thinking about" was the question of "survival or integrity"[11]; and the same idea informs his elaborate reviews of Chaplin's *Monsieur Verdoux*. For Agee, Verdoux was, as has been noted, a metaphor for the condition of man in a society in which business and love had become rigidly separated: "Verdoux has done what many of us have done. He has concluded that all that is best in him and dearest to him can be preserved only by the exercise of all that is worst."[12] When preparing the review of *Verdoux*, Agee's hopes for America were dismal: "at present by con-

siderable odds the most nauseating country on the face of the earth;
. . . sinking still lower day by day; and may be expected reasonably
soon, to fall straight into strict moral oblivion."

His concern about the drift of society and individualism emerges
from additional articles written for *Time*. Two unpublished essays
treat the problem of acting responsibly in a world where *unin-
dividualistic* ideas had become a form of "Popular Religion."[13] The
first of these articles is prefaced by "Consider the lilies of the
field. . . ." Agee then asserts that, while most persons in the
Western world are nominally Christians, "the world's history, and
the daily and future destiny of every individual, are given shape,
meanwhile, by . . . trivial assumptions, taboos, fears, prejudices
which men in effective numbers believe so fully that they act accordingly." Such malformed opinions ranged from views about the
"nobleness" of war and "democracy" to the conviction that groups
and races can be guilty as such, or that it is possible "to enjoy the
benefits of materialism without being liable to its hazards." Such
beliefs motivated Western man's action, and seldom did men act
out of clear conviction or religious faith; they more often adopted
the incorrect thoughts of other groups.

The second article, written for the 1945 Christmas issue of *Time*,
is a meditation about how all men bear the Christ child in their
hearts. The typed manuscript is heavily edited (whether or not by
Agee is impossible to know), and the Christmas issue contained only
a short version of Agee's draft, along with a quotation of scripture.
Because the original version of the story must have seemed controversial, and because it is such a beautifully formed statement of
how difficult it is to live as a Christian in the world, it bears examination: ". . . Christ is born again: a Child who may stand for
all that is most brave, most innocent, most loving, most generous,
most kin to the divine in all men, whether Christians or not."[14]
Christmas is the time of the manifestation of the child in
man—trust and innocence. But not only is the child born again:
"For each of us must recognize in himself not only the Child, but
also the Mother and the Foster-Father, the Shepherds and the
Magi, the Angels and the Beast, and Herod, as well." When Agee
asked "What is this child!" he answered: "He is all that each man
knows in the best conscience of his own soul, and all that has the
humility and the courage to try to act accordingly, without com-

promise, against no matter what pressures or inducements. A non-religious word for this is individualism." This consideration of the presence of Christ is also a meditation about the difficulty of acting at all in a world full of evil. Although Agee wrote little poetry during these years, he includes these same ideas in verse. In a poem entitled "Christmas 1945" he wrote

> Once more, as in the ancient morning,
> The slow beasts, the fierce new-born cry;
> And, in the heart the dreadful warning:
>   Is it I?[15]

This poem synthesizes his conviction that individual peace is the primary need of men if they are to live in a fragmented modern world. No doubt this poem and the unused version for *Time* magazine were both written with similar conviction and enthusiasm. Significantly, Agee's own desire to act as an individual gave rise to the most productive period in his career.

II *"Dedication Day"*

These convictions relative to individualism were intensified by the horrors of the atomic bomb, for, to Agee, the war and the cynicism connected with it had been too easily accepted by Americans. His most succinct literary treatment of the demise of individualism is the satire "Dedication Day, a rough sketch for a motion picture." This bitter account satirizes the imagined dedication of a monument designed to commemorate the discovery of the atom's destructive power. As a parody of journalistic methods, the opening paragraphs, reprinted in *The Collected Short Prose*, amass facts to document the event reported; but there are no directions for the use of camera. If this work were truly a sketch for a film, some minimal suggestions for camera use would have been included.

The sketch falls into two sections; the ceremony and one particular incident. The dedication was of an "heroic new Arch which was for all time to come to memorialize the greatest of human achievements,"[16] and representatives from all countries and all faiths attended the grotesque ceremony which took place between the Washington obelisk and the Lincoln Memorial. The reporter sarcastically castigates (among other things) Catholic Cardinals,

Boy Scouts, American legislators, and the misuse of Beethoven's Ninth Symphony. Gathered at the base of the "fused uranium" monument are peoples from all parts of the world who pay unthinking reverence to a force they cannot understand. The rhythmic prose suggests the mesmerization under which the crowd has been placed; and the minutely detailed account of the ceremony catalogues the mores and false gods which Agee abhorred in modern civilization: ". . . in perfect synchronization the military bands of forty-six nations and the National Broadcasting Symphony Orchestra and the Westminster Choir attacked respectively their respective national anthems . . ." (107). As the sketch develops, the reporter's bitterness grows in intensity and his fears about individualism become more apparent.

In the second part, which reveals the planning of the memorial, the most grotesque aspects of Agee's imagination are brought sharply into focus. The entire monument, its design and maintenance as well as its dedication, are the result of hypocrisy and delusion; and only one person, a physicist who had been involved in the development of the bomb, emerges as admirable. He repudiates what others meekly, foolishly, and maliciously accept; but the reporter fails, of course, to understand this fact. The physicist had "begun, not long after the Japanese surrender, to strike his colleagues as a little queer. . . . He was known to have attended Mass, at first secretly, then quite openly . . . asked Mahatma Gandhi's postal address . . ." (112). Later the "deranged" scientist asked to work with the deformed survivors of the bombings when it was known they would be weaving a wick for the Memorial's torch—a fuse calculated to burn at the rate of one inch per second, the sound of which would grow continuously "more acute never dynamically more loud": its cotton was to be provided from a special "Sharecropper's Rehabilitation Project." The explanation that the fuse would burn at the rate of "an inch per second" is a matter-of-fact report about the result of careful planning for economic problems.

The suicide of the physicist climaxes the sketch, for he took poison as he threw a switch to ignite the eternal fuse. He obviously did so because he felt guilty; but the persona, through whom the sketch is presented, interprets his suicide as madness. Even before that incident, while the physicist had been on "view," tourists were able to see that his speech was a "blended stream of self-vilification and of pr-y-r" (113). His final act (Agee's reporter ironically suggests) is an example of "the unfortunate effects of a single man's unbridled individualism."

"Dedication Day" clearly is closer to a parody of a news story than to an outline for a movie. Minute and meaningless details are amassed: "Within a few minutes after Dedication he was found next the great spool, dead by his own hand (by prussic acid)." The sketch stands as an indictment of a society in which any act of courage or heroism can be interpreted as a deviation from the norm.

III *Private Writings*

Not surprisingly, little formal poetry was written by Agee during these years, and the attempts he did make at writing verse reveal a troubled mind. His poems demonstrate both disappointment with the contemporary world and his own fear of failure as artist, but his personal dissatisfaction is most evident in the poems he left unpublished. Two sonnets written to commemorate his birthday in 1945 are representative. A variant of the first of these has subsequently appeared in the *Collected Poems*, but both were originally published in *The Texas Quarterly*. At age thirty-six, Agee wrote:

> Now on the world and on my life as well,
> Ancient in beauty, infant in such fear
> As no time else had dreamed, nor shall dispel,
> Loosen the ashes of another year.
> Whether by nature's will, man's or my own,
> I who by chance walked softly past a war
> Shall not by any chance the world has known
> Be here, and breathing, many autumns more.
> Only, with all who in past worlds have died,
> I had, till lately, faced my death secure,
> Knowing my hunger only was denied;
> All I most loved and honored would endure.
> But this year, dying, struck wild as it fell,
> Ending itself, me, and the world as well.[17]

The poignancy of his personal suffering implies that it is part of a greater cycle: ". . . on the world and on [his] life as well, . . . Loosen the ashes of another year"—another reference to the atomic bomb. Personal disappointment and frustration dominate the companion poem:

> O long, long, idle in tribulation,
> Grown fat in all I did because I must,
> I dreamed at least I knew my own salvation:
> Now I begin to wake, and it is dust.
> Where is the Angel in whose rage alone
> Wrestling, I live? The night is nearly gone.[18]

Middle age brought disappointment to the hopefulness of the younger poet, and Agee complains of his inability to find a means to prove himself. Earlier, he had felt that through artistic work he could be redeemed. The ambiguous "I dreamed at least I knew my own salvation" seems to refer to both earlier religious and artistic convictions; but, after reviewing his accomplishments, Agee found little for comfort.

This unpublished verse was occasioned by a decade of the worst war in history, an era which might be approached by laughter; but for someone as meditative as Agee the sterility of society could not be joked about for long. He began another poem by writing: "Marx, I agree. Einstein, I partly follow./ Keep your seats please. I'm everybody's friend." But the immediately following lines alter the tone: "And yet I find it hollow, hollow, hollow/ And only wish tonight might be the end."[19] Too many disappointments are encountered, and the possibility of not accomplishing artistic aspirations looms large:

> Rivers inscribe their trees: the listing earth
> Retires, restores, its halves upon the sun:
> Continually I hear the shouts of birth,
> The sighs of death, and I wish that I were done.
>
> All things amaze me and the time seems great
> With joy and wisdom scarcely yet described.
> The chains and emblems of the ghastly State
> Rust off: the race, the earth, are groom and bride.

Birth is not joyful, a "shout" to be endured on a "listing" planet where death brings a "sigh" of relief.

When Agee composed this poem, he felt that few of his aspirations were to be realized. His image of the state's disintegration and his plea for a wedding between man and world is a call for death: "Yet must I drown beneath a depth of dreams/ And never hope for any breathing more." The main disappointment which Agee seemed incapable of facing was that he could not achieve his artistic goals; he seemed unable to put his vision into words. He wrote: "All I care to live for is to show/ These [experiences of the world] as they seem. To see, and not to say."

He also composed a group of four sonnets, two of which were published in 1947, which also delineate his fears about his wasted talent. Each of these employs a variation on the Bellerophon theme. The first asks "Who was that boy, ranging the ruined hill,/ Spine humbled to the horse's huge, light ghost," who killed his winged carrier? [20] The related three sonnets reply that the killer is the speaker who cannot fathom why he allowed himself to kill the poetic power which had formerly supported him.

One poem published by Agee in 1949, a lullaby, purports that only in the sleep of the small child is peace found; for agony comes with maturity. The lullaby is suggestive both of what Agee suffered and of the condition of the world. He wrote at least two other lullabies—one now published, the other in manuscript—which parallel the thoughts of the 1949 poem. In the unpublished poem, a song is sung for the perhaps unborn sleeping child, probably his daughter Teresa.

> If in your dreams you hear, forgive:
> For by our doing you must live.
>
> Soon you must wake, and dreams be done
> When you behold the heavy sun.
>
> Once you undertake that weight,
> Apologies will come too late. [21]

Despite the fact that creative powers were absorbed by critical writing and by concerns about his contemporary world, Agee continued his imaginative writing. His autographical "1928 Story," written in the mid-1940s, is about his disillusionment and unhappiness, but it also demostrates that he could evoke earlier remembered times. A continued interest in the past eventually led to *The Morning Watch* and *A Death in the Family*; and among unpublished materials, his notes exist for three stories about adolescence, all of which are similar and outlined for film treatment. The third story was "somewhat less clearly shaped and more psychologically entangled and is perhaps more amenable to literary than to movie treatment, but of that I'm not sure. Each of the heroes in stories 1 and 2 have a certain coherence and distinctness of grace; the focus here would be more on adolescent incoherence, inconsistency, unpredictability, and the blend of grace with gracelessness, and would work more closely within more complicated emotions."[22] "1928 Story" is a fictional treatment of adolescence.

Still another incomplete project involves writing based on inference. In 1937, Agee outlined a way to develop writing which would rely upon the use of the imagination to reveal what one knew only indirectly.[23] Thus, Buenos Aires, or West Virginia, could be written about by those who had never been there; he suggested that a history of the Civil War might be constructed in such a manner; and a varied set of working manuscripts reveals his own attempts. He wrote a short story set in the Civil War, as well as some dramatization accompanied by poetry.[24] Perhaps he felt the project could be adapted for film, for he mentioned showing a Civil War story to at least one producer. The manuscript story, which evokes the imagined atmosphere of a battlefield, is similar in its method of specificity to the style of *A Death in the Family* and of later screen plays. Moreover, the evocation of a single moment suggests·wider meaning: one bird's disturbance suggests the suffering of many. The manuscript fragments about the Civil War, the one war in American history which he did not find repulsive, show his attempts to make some order of the horror of war through art. His final fiction is a development of the same method. There, as in "1928 Story," he ordered the memories of his own life.

CHAPTER 7

"*Screen-Writing as Literature*"

I

A GEE began writing scripts in somewhat the same way he did criticism during his earlier years: he chose to do both because, in theory, they allowed a degree of freedom and time for other writing. Although in 1948 he left *Time* so that he could do more of his own work, *A Death in the Family* remained unfinished at his death seven years later because he was drawn into so many film projects. In an article written during the early 1950s, Agee commented on his change from film critic to screenwriter. It seemed to him "elementary that many critics are, as naturally, artists"; but he acknowledged that "the duties of the artist and the critic differ fundamentally."[1] He noted the critic must understand the work before him, but "the business of an artist is even more simply to give the specific task all the best he has in him." If the artist properly proportions his work, then it will possess "vitality, and harmony, and integrity."

Agee did acknowledge that the scriptwriter's work was only part of an elaborate procedure wherein many artists and technicians collaborated; a moviewriter might hope for praise, but "movies were so intricately collaborative that it is impossible to assign personal praise or dispraise correctly." Yet he himself wrote scripts as if the ideas and suggestions, as committed to paper, were the final product. The result of such a procedure was finally frustration, for it took several years of scriptwriting for him to realize fully that doing screenplays was much like journalism for *Fortune*. Apparently, he was confident about his many film ideas; and he does not seem to have faced the real problem of how much energy he should put into scriptwriting.

A revealing example of the scope of his film hopes is the

manuscript for the projected film "Scientists and Tramps" which he conceived as a vehicle for his favorite actor and film maker, Charlie Chaplin. In this projected film Agee imagines society as reconstructing itself after the "Ultimate Bomb" has exploded. The mood of the proposed work lacks the bitterness of the satire "Dedication Day," and "Scientists and Tramps" suggests what might be possible if man could again act as an individual; and the symbol for that individualism is Chaplin's tramp. The film would begin with a "comic political-scientific prologue";[2] the bomb would be dropped; and most of the world would be devastated. The balance of the film would trace the rebuilding of civilization around two camps—the scientific and the individualistic; additional scenes would alternate between each camp; and eventually the " 'Forces for Good,' " the dominant scientific powers which Agee satirizes would regain dominance. Agee wanted the film to be a satire about contemporary attitudes toward science; and he also wanted to show, under proper conditions, the possibilities for childlike qualities of love and trust to reassert themselves. The tramp's trust, openness, and childlikeness would have encouraged others to rediscover lost virtues in themselves.

The working draft of "Scientists and Tramps" runs to sixty-six pages; however, little more than notes were completed. Some dialogue was projected; several scenes outlined; but only the prologue was worked out in detail. That prologue was to be made from newsreel clips and was to be accompanied by a satirical speech by a speaker who embodied The American Politician. The harangue by the "Grand Old Man," a beautiful example of the parody Agee relished, illustrates what occurs if people pretend they are individuals when they are only unthinking followers. Basic to the Old Man's character is an ability to pretend he is thinking when only talking. (An analogous phenomenon is "pseudo-folk" art which, through ignorance and stupidity, is accepted as the real thing. Agee's ideas about such art are outlined in an article published in 1944, but similar ideas are reflected in "Popular Religion.")[3] The irony of the opening speech, which quickly gives way to pathos, is the speaker's apparent belief in what he says; but his inability to examine what he is saying is indicated by his clouded rhetoric.

The ending of the Old Man's speech was to coincide with the explosion of the "Ultimate Bomb," the opening of the main part of the film. The prologue and the cheers with which the speech is accepted indicate that Americans are incapable of deciding against the bomb. One is reminded of Agee's fascination with "The Roosevelt Story," a film which made him realize "that a terrifying number of Americans, most of them in all innocence of the fact, are much more ripe for benevolent dictatorship . . . than for the most elementary realization of the meanings, hopes, and liabilities of democracy."[4] With such ideas in mind, "Scientists and Tramps" was planned; and many scenes were outlined or sketched. Agee knew the difficulty in maintaining the right spirit for such a film: the personal story of the tramp could be easily dramatized, but showing "what goodness does to power" would be much more difficult. Also "in [a] relatively good community the tramp can hardly any longer function as the tramp. We see for the first time how thoroughly he has depended upon being an outcast." Agee's hopes for this project were vast, and his detailed notes might be compared to a dream which draws together criticism of society and hopes for film making, a combination of comedy and parable. Whether he ever talked with a producer about the film is unknown.

Still another project, but one which is admired because it accomplishes its goal, is a documentary for which Agee wrote commentary in 1947. His first filmscript to be actually produced, it was a collaboration with Helen Levitt; and, entitled *The Quiet One*, it is about a Harlem boy who is sent to a reformatory. This modest documentary continues to be shown in the 1970s because many suggestions Agee made over the years through his criticism are utilized in it. *The Quiet One* uses sustained sequences of Harlem to contribute to its mood. Donald, the main character, has no dialogue, but Agee's narration makes his loneliness felt. Donald's freedom to wander in the city was a kind of solitary confinement, and his loneliness is conveyed by commentary and shots of the child wandering the streets. At the conclusion of the manuscript, Agee appended for his commentary pages of notes about sound and cutting. Above all, he wanted to utilize the sound and rhythm of the city atmosphere which made the young hero feel lonely.

II *Adaptations*

Agee thought of screenwriting as a means to obtain money so that he might do other writing; but, after he suffered a series of heart attacks in 1951, he wrote to Father Flye to indicate his depression over the "very little" he had accomplished since he had left *Time* three years earlier. He admitted that his health was a serious problem and that he knew whether he lived and accomplished what he wished to accomplish "depends on whether or not I can learn to be the kind of person I am not and have always detested."[5] He recognized that he had to learn discipline. His scriptwriting, only an intermediary step in film production, was simply a job since the screen ideas usually did not originate with him; he was called in to visualize a story and to arrange the dialogue.[6] Most of the film work, therefore, did not allow either the latitude for his imagination as in "Scientists and Tramps" or of his imaginative use of setting and amateur actors as in *The Quiet One*. An adaptation imposes limitations on the scenarist who must adhere to the spirit of the original, and Agee himself had often raised objections about the use of a literary text in a film if it became a source of distraction. He understood that adaptations must have an independent life, and he had already demonstrated a decade earlier his meticulousness with such a project with his adaptation of Malraux's *Man's Fate*.

Agee's scripts are conceived like novels. The reliance upon the first-person plural in directions is a novelist's point of view.[7] In many instances Agee provides so much detail and suggestion that little is left for the imagination of the director. Gerald Weales has observed that it is "comic and a little sad" that Agee's small body of film work should consist mostly of adaptations when he himself "longed to see movies free themselves from their literary dependence," but this comment overlooks Agee's gift for visualizing detail.[8] Agee felt compelled to go beyond retelling the story, and his scripts can be described, because of their elaborate suggestions for gesture, sound, and camera use, as the production of a frustrated director.

The similarity of theme in each adaptation indicates that Agee must have exercised discretion in choosing projects; for in each case, he chose a literary work in which the regenerate or unregenerate Adamic motif is basic. He was fascinated with the idea of the confrontation of innocence with evil—a situation which is immediately obvious in both of the Stephen Crane stories for which he did scripts, "The Blue Hotel" and "The Bride Comes to Yellow Sky." In the first, an intruder breaks up the peacefulness of a prairie town; in the other, Potter brings his bride home, and it becomes clear that the town troublemaker will leave. *The African Queen* is a love story "Edenic both in setting and its values,"[9] and thematic parallels are evident between *The Night of the Hunter* and *Huckleberry Finn*. Lastly, Gauguin's diaries, *Noa Noa*, from which Agee drew film materials, are essentially the record of an artist's break with civilization in an attempt to find peace in a primitive setting.

Agee's adaptations are faithful to both the words and spirit of his sources, as in the case of both Crane adaptations.[10] In "The Blue Hotel" Agee condensed or transposed material, but his additions "are simply matters of expanding the characterizations." The Swede's behavior during supper is described in one paragraph by Crane while in Agee five pages emphasize this character's overconfidence, but the result establishes a clearer rhythm for the film. Several paragraphs of camera directions are also provided for a transitional scene from the hotel to the fight outside it. In Agee's adaptation of "The Bride Comes to Yellow Sky," the emphasis is on the breakdown of the code of the West; and this script has been called "Agee's finest piece of writing for the screen, and a work of genuine charm."[11] If so, it is because he is attentive to details, for, even when Agee relied very heavily upon Crane's story, he wrote elaborate directions for camera use. When Potter and his bride are introduced, Agee suggests that "for a few moments we merely HOLD on them, as though this were a provincial wedding portrait of the period. (Circa 1895) He has an outdoor clumsiness in his new suit, which is a shade tight and small for him. Her very new-looking hat and dress are in touchingly ambitious, naive taste."[12]

"The Bride Comes to Yellow Sky" is considerably expanded from the Crane story. In Crane's version, the salesman has little to say; in the adaptation, he becomes a major character. The bartender in Crane's story becomes a woman in the script, and humor between Potter and his bride is added. Almost all of Crane's dialogue was used, but a fundamental change occurs in emphasis. Scratchy, the town troublemaker seems much more sinister in the story. In the film, additions result in a lighter tone which suggests a frontier settlement that is rapidly changing from a village to a sedate, respectable small town. The gunfight between Scratchy and Potter comes to nothing; the hardness of frontier life is gone.

The first full-length script which Agee wrote which was subsequently produced is *The African Queen*. Because of the
collaborative nature of Hollywood films and also because Agee's
work was interrupted by illness, it is difficult to attribute an exact
portion of the work on this script to him. Because extensive
manuscripts do exist, however, it is possible to determine which portions originated with Agee. John Huston wrote minimal detailed
description of action; but, in Agee's sections, as might be suspected,
considerable detail is provided. Agee's opening scene is an example
of sound and image intricately supporting each other: the church
service, with its organ, and the congregation dressed in glaring
white provides a contrast. The scene which immediately follows, in
which Rose, her brother, and Allnutt have tea is an addition which
Agee made for the film; for no comparable scene exists in C. S.
Forester's novel. Typically, Agee wrote more than a full page of
directions about sound and gesture for this short scene.

Agee's screenplays go beyond being director's notes; they provide
dialogue with a commentary on individual images. Barson suggests
that Agee's scripts, properly considered, resemble visually rendered
novels, and scenes such as either of these opening ones in *The
African Queen* support that assertion. Another aspect of Agee's influence on the making of *The African Queen* was his anticipation of
its need for a distinguishing rhythm. He admired Huston's
photography and the power conveyed through good camera work,
but he felt that the overall rhythm of Huston's work might be im-
proved. In writing the falls sequences of *The African Queen*, "Agee
wanted to create the illusion of one, unbroken shot of danger after
danger";[13] and the effect was to be a mounting series of suspenseful
scenes. Relief for the audience comes only from Rose and Charley's
efforts to run the current.

Another work which Agee adapted from novel to film was Davis
Grubb's *The Night of the Hunter*, and the adaptation again relies
heavily upon the source. In the screenplay, which catches the night-
marish confrontation of innocence with evil, the story concerns Ben
Harper, who is executed because he killed two men in a bank
robbery. Before he is hanged, his cellmate "Preacher" Harry Powell
tries to learn the hiding place of the money. Unsuccessful, Powell
goes to Ben's family, torments them, and kills his widow, Willa. The
children, John, age nine, and Pearl, age five, escape on the river and

eventually find a haven. Agee succeeds in capturing the quietness of the river settings and his script sustains its "delicate balance between adult nightmare and childhood vision. It is perhaps one of the two or three finest 'horror' movies produced in the last two decades."[14] Thematically similarities are apparent between the film and Agee's own autobiographical novel: the basic theme of Grubb's novel, the innocence of children contrasted with the evil of the Preacher, is similar to the theme of innocence confronting death in *A Death in the Family.*

Agee's film script *Noa Noa* has not been produced, and opinions about it range from the extremely positive to negative. The scenario, his most fully detailed one, is the record of the artist Paul Gauguin's attempt to get away from civilization. Gauguin's son, Emile, commented that the story reflects "a true understanding of his father's spirit and courage";[15] but many critics, however, feel it is weak. Commentators suggested that *Noa Noa* was for Agee a summing-up of his career and of his concept of the artistic impulse which derives from suffering; and this view of the artist resulted in his sentimentalizing Gauguin's role. Fitzgerald writes that "in all Agee's work the worst example of this is . . . *Noa Noa*, and anyone can see [it] becoming at times a maudlin caricature of the artist-as-saint."

The script emphasizes the role of the individual and his search for lost innocence, and Agee relied heavily upon Gauguin's journal, sometimes following it word for word; but he also utilized his awareness of sound, camera angles, light, and dialogue in the creation of an overall rhythm. Such detail necessitated elaborate explanatory material; and, as Agee noted in a letter to David Bradley, the proposed director for *Noa Noa*, his scripts tended to be longer than usual because of an "excessive and unconvention[al] amount of . . . direction."[16] The result is, as Pechter phrases it, "what is best in Agee's writing for screen remains less part of the history of art than that of suggestion, speculation, aspiration, passionate desire, and the ephemera of dreams."[17]

What *Noa Noa* best demonstrates is Agee's sense of particularity of character and his attempt to use many cinematic techniques to this purpose. The draft notes for *Noa Noa* indicate how various techniques might be combined: "without any major distortion, from his own style, [and] away from the 'documentary'; we must always be able to carry our own perception, and Gauguin's figure and reactions, in balance. . . . "[18] Although descriptions of scenes are quite detailed, Agee cannot verbalize all he imagined; for example, at one point before paragraphs which describe a crucial scene he has apologetically written, "Fully to detail the shots for this sequence would type out deceptively long, so the action—which involves 40 seconds—is only outlined here."[19]

III   *Other Film Projects*

Agee worked on many other projects during the last years of his life, some of which were produced. Other material remains in manuscript or was only sketched, and three of these are representative pieces that demonstrate his interests. The Omnibus series about Lincoln, a screenplay about a musical festival which was finished, and a brief sketch for a film included in his final letter to Flye reveal the range of his projects.

Agee's five-part presentation for "Omnibus" about Abraham Lincoln was, in the words of Mayer Levin, "the most original and important work so far created for video."[20] The focus was upon Lincoln's desire "to find himself, to assert himself against the violence of life in his pioneer surroundings [and to show] his own passionate love for all that lives: his own tenderness."[21] This television series met with critical success; and, after production, the film was reedited and shown as a regular-length movie. The filming was done on location to emphasize the peculiarly American characteristics of Lincoln's background. In a pencil note for an introduction to the series, Agee wrote that the programs were meant to show "how a child born into the humblest depth . . . began to ripen into one of the greatest men who ever lived . . . and how many of the things . . . which gave him his shape, were new in the world, and unique to this nation." The theme of a great man who came from an ordinary setting provided an exceptionally good chance for Agee, and he made the most of it. Since the new medium of television allowed him to emphasize semidocumentary methods, the film opens with shots of the funeral train as it moved from Washington to Illinois, for which Agee provided extensive notes so that its nineteenth-century setting would be suggested.

Plans for a feature-length film *Tanglewood Story*, about five or six musicians who study at the Boston Symphony's Tanglewood

Festival, seemed equally promising for many documentary methods. In an outline letter about this project, Agee noted that "at its dead center the film is simply about art and . . . vocation: about music, and musicians. . . . it is a film about the human spirit, or soul, and about the courage, and grace of God (i.e., talent or genius) which must combine to serve the human soul."[22] The Tanglewood film, as written, became neither the story of persons who fall in love and happen to be musicians, nor the story of musicians who fall in love while they are perfecting musical skills. Instead, the story is about at least six different musicians who became enamored of one another while they perfect their musical talents;[23] and the result is a lack of focus. Although completed and purchased by a large studio, it was never produced. Apparently the screenplay developed into a more complicated series of relationships than could be handled easily.

Another movie idea, outlined in a letter, concerns the capture and abuse of elephants. Moving from fantasy to fact, the film would have begun with an address by a disembodied "voice of God" informing elephants who have converged from all over Africa that a new age is about to begin. Then would have followed a series of episodes about the abuse of circus elephants with a grand finale in ballet, which George Balanchine instructs and which elephants perform. Dwight Macdonald implies that these insights, Agee's last ones to be recorded on paper, suggest that he saw a parallel between himself and the great beasts which were misused;[24] but to make such an assumption seems presumptious. What is significant is that Agee continued to imagine motion pictures until just a few days before his death.

CHAPTER 8

Short Fiction

I

I N the 1940s, Agee's creative work was devoted mostly to writing about or for films, but he continued to hope that he could do other writing. In 1943, he wrote Dwight Macdonald "I am at present in difficulty what with this and that: this meaning this book I am trying to write, and that meaning that book I am trying to write."[1] In 1945, he began a novel "about adolescence" which was not, as has been mistakenly assumed, *The Morning Watch*.[2] During this same year, he also began both a story and a book about the atomic bomb for which apparently no manuscript survives.[3] Manuscript notes indicate that he worked also on adaptations of Shakespeare's *Macbeth* and of Greek tragedies, either for film or fictional treatment.[4] So many projects dissipated his energy.

Another example of Agee as a person who put perhaps too much energy into the project at hand is his tape-recorded letter made for Father Flye in 1953.[5] He described in it some of the projects in which he was involved including the option of making a film of *Moby Dick* with John Huston or of directing a film on location in the Philippines. But interestingly a significant portion of this impromptu voice-letter is devoted to relating how a rabbit had been attacked by a dog near his house. Agee's description of the animal's fear and the visit to the veterinarian reveal his empathy and his ability to concentrate on an event close at hand. His fascination with the beauty of that moment and his enjoyment in retelling it are reflected in his unrehearsed words in which the commonplace is made to shine. Agee regularly maintained that such artistry was possible; but, because of journalism or film demands, he did not often attempt to capture the texture of everyday events as he had in *Famous Men*. His mature short fiction demonstrates a renewed con-

cern with how simple events reveal meaning when properly apprehended. His respect for "the dignity of actuality" therefore
generated fiction which reflects a carefully observed world and
which exemplifies the use of imagination to evoke the complexity of
ordinary events.

II *A Fable*

In the fall of 1951, Agee wrote the stark fable "A Mother's Tale,"
sometimes interpreted as a symbolic statement about his own life.
Such overtones may be present, for it would have been impossible
for him to compose "A Mother's Tale" and be unaware of parallels
with the way his own energy had been consumed in distractions
from serious artistic endeavors. But the tale is chiefly an allegory
about man in a controlled society; in fact, "A Mother's Tale," as
allegory, provides commentary on man's herd instinct. Many of its
ideas are obviously similar to earlier attacks on modern civilization
expressed in his works like "Dedication Day" and his projected
"Scientists and Tramps." But the fable is far more appealing than
"Dedication Day" because an understanding of man's weakness is
apparent. This fable, reprinted in *The Collected Short Prose of
James Agee*, emphasizes the innocence and gullibility of all men. A
mother cow relates to her son how a steer once came back from the
slaughterhouse and urged others to be aware of "the true ultimate
purpose of man."[6] The One Who Came Back preached that "*Each
one is himself*" and that all fences should be destroyed (240).

Any belief that One really did return is not widespread. The
narrator can recall only vaguely the strains of a song "Great-
grandmother used to sing . . . 'Be not like dumb-driven cattle
. . .' "; and, while the great-grandmother had received her information about the One Who Came Back from a direct witness, the
mother tells her son: "you couldn't always be sure she knew quite
what she was saying" because she "was so very, very old you see"
(242 and 226). This dialogue functions like David Hume's argument
against the validity of traditional religion; yet, presented within the
context of the fable, the fact that each person demands to learn for
himself emphasizes man's weakness.

The tone is ironic. The mother reveals what the One Who Came

Back had told earlier members of the herd, but she does not understand why she is compelled to relate such horror. Why should she
tell a story about how cattle are rounded up and forced to ride in
wooden boxes over steel bands to a mysterious place, then forced to
walk a corridor to confront Him, the one with the hammer? Such a
myth may only frighten listeners. Nevertheless, she tells about the
One Who Came Back, and how by perseverance he found his way
home to reveal what happens to the herded. That message included
an admonition to destroy the young and to refuse to cooperate with
those who use cattle. The One Who Came Back announced: "*We
are brought into this life only to be victims; and there is no other
way for us unless we save ourselves*" (241). Although individuals do
suffer at the hands of others, the listening calf insists upon discover-
ing the truth for himself because of the impossibility of his deter-
mining if the narrator believes the tale.

The mother-narrator cannot understand why life should contain
mysteries like railroads and slaughterhouses; and, rather than
believe the words of the prophet, she shrugs them off as untruthful.
When her calf insists that she say if she believes she replies: " 'Of
course not, silly,' . . . and all at once she was overcome by a most
curious shyness, for it occured to her that in the course of time, this
young thing might be bred to her. 'It's just an old, old legend.'
With a tender little laugh she added, lightly, 'We use it to frighten
children with' " (242). With this self-indictment, the tale becomes
most frightening. Mothers encourage sons to be bright and to work
hard, and the brightest are allowed to stay home. The irony, of
course, is that such escape represents no salvation. Staying at home
is only another contribution to the system, and those who stay allow
others to be rounded up and sent to the cities.

As the fable progresses, Agee suggests several levels of meaning.
The message of the One, " '*Each one is himself. . . . Not one of
the herd. . . . Himself alone . . . if even a few do not hear me, or
disbelieve me, we are all betrayed*' " (240), encapsulates Agee's dissatisfaction with modern life, which is so organized that it seems impossible to escape. Analogies between the tale and the family structure, economics, and war each present themselves; and in each instance, a few advance through the destruction of others.

Agee, essentially, lets his reader draw the necessary conclusions.
The reports of the cattle herded into ugly wagons (so crowded that

they cannot lie down) suggest persons forced into cars to be sent to concentration camps. The One Who Came Back reported that on his journey a passenger train was passed and one of the human faces seemed to indicate that he understood at least a little bit: "One . . . looked into his eyes and smiled, as if he liked him, or as if he knew only too well how hard the journey was" (229); and Agee's reader realizes that he, too, has smiled. The cities to which cattle are taken symbolize the mistakes man perpetrated in his greed which consumes goods and people. The slaughterhouse where animals are destroyed smells "Like old fire . . . and old blood and fear and darkness and sorrow and most terrible and brutal force . . ." (231).

"A Mother's Tale" laments the shortsightedness of man. Its characters remain very much animals, but everything is written to suggest that man is both murderer and victim. Agee arranges his tale so that the reader feels sympathy for beasts; but the reader slowly realizes that he himself is a member of the herd and that suffering, even death itself, is not to be fully explained. But, if death is inexplicable, life is to be lived to the fullest, as the One Who Came Back urges. To submit without question, or to be used without asserting one's individuality, is tragic. Agee's mature fiction continues to develop these ideas—the inexplicability of death along with the ambiguity and celebration of living; but in other fiction he concentrates more upon the beauty of living.

III   *Return to Biography*

His partly autobiographical "1928 Story" probably was completed during the late 1940s, for it begins with an evocation of mood similar to that of some of the unpublished poetry of those years, and it also includes a cynicism similar to that of "Dedication Day." But it resembles in technique and in nostalgic tone the later autobiographical fiction. "1928 Story" catches the spontaneity, enthusiasm, and confusion of an adolescent, and the story has value because it indicates significant facts about the mature Agee. First, it again embodies his ambivalent attitude about the role of the "artist": possibly any artist is "immature." Second, Agee's first sustained attempt after *Famous Men* to recreate a mood from his own life is at the core of "1928 Story."[7]

Although, as has been indicated, exact dating of "1928 Story" is impossible; the internal evidence suggests the years immediately following the war. It might be part of the novel "about adolescence" which Agee mentioned in a letter of November, 1945. [8] The inference that his letter refers to *The Morning Watch* is incorrect because the later novella has as its central character a boy of only twelve, and *The Morning Watch* was written in 1950. The hero of "1928 Story" is an adolescent. As the story opens Irvine, a writer, listens to old records which remind him of his much earlier years when the same music had been heard in an altogether different atmosphere, one affected by adolescent confidence and hope as an aspiring artist. Irvine's wife associates the same music with times just before the war; therefore, she is reminded of different events. Irvine realizes that his dwelling on his earliest associations with the music is "a way of retreating from her"; but his inability to feel "trust or hope in anything" makes it difficult for him to live in the present (23). The interior monologue suggests the apparent meaninglessness of convictions which Irvine has maintained, and it quickly drifts into an account of his present listless mood. He is obsessed with the conviction that he might have produced more creditable work; but his lack of confidence has made it nearly impossible for him to write. As the story continues in a flashback, he remembers "suddenly, with incredible sadness," a morning "when confidence was abundant" (26); and the remainder of the story is a presentation of that confidence and adolescent feelings.

What the story suggests is that no moment can really be clear; all become clouded by myriad emotions and reactions. The remembrance of an earlier state of mind is central to the story. To suggest the way he feels during the present, as compared with some twenty years earlier, a specific incident about his seeing a girl on the beach and about his reaction to her is elaborated. What is implied in this recollection is that the confidence of adolescence stems largely from inexperience. The young Irvine's sure acceptance of his role as artist is emphasized—in his deliberations about compositions; in his imaginative conception about musicians; and in the poetic tribute which ends the story. With maturity, Irvine sees some of the foolishness of his youthful hopes. His adolescent manner, however, was also beautiful—and it remains pleasurable to recall the simplicities of that state.

The melancholy of Irvine is vividly caught by the contrast with his attitude of the earlier period. The mature writer lost practically all interest and confidence in his work; all of his hopes, for himself and for the world, appear to have come to nothing. Only "meanness . . . fatness, and insanity, seemed to survive. . . . It was a stupefied country, and evidently a stupefied world, and as stupefied as anything else was his sense of universal mistrust and of hopeless regret . . . (24)." As the mature writer looks back at his earlier buoyant confidence, while realizing his adolescent inabilities, he cannot help but mourn the death of his earlier confidence. He remembers only too well when "it was going to be a wonderful summer." At times, the prose captures the immediacy of that remembered event; and objects, such as the cottages on the beach, are described for what appears to be their own sake. And such admiration of reality permeates the description and gives understanding of the sadness of the older Irvine.

In contrast to the hopes of adolescence, the mature Irvine realistically sees that he had been incapable of judging either his experiences with a girl or his ability to poeticize the experience. The poem which concludes the story is an ironic commentary upon the ideals of a young artist who wanted to be a James Joyce. Trite epiphany and harsh rhythm combine to emphasize its mediocrity:

> Where I waited, listlessly
> On Summer's unportentuous brink,
> You stepped up out of the sea
> Now I can no longer think. (37)

Even the young Irvine realized that "he had seldom written a worse poem"; yet he did not destroy it. He at least had the confidence to write. The mature Irvine, aware that his apparent talent had not been what he hoped, no longer has much confidence.

IV *Evocation of St. Andrew's*

The Morning Watch (1951), a novella, is the first fully successful attempt of Agee to turn his back on the confusion of his own life and to recreate a remembered moment. Much like Joyce's *A Portrait of the Artist as a Young Man*, Agee's novella catches the beauty of a hero confronted by different and conflicting drives, motives, and passions. Its twelve-year-old hero experiences a high point of religious emotion, but that moment is an ironic one. Indeed, *The Morning Watch* achieves success because of its focus upon a pinnacle of religious fervor which the reader senses must inevitably diminish. The book is about the special hours of the Maundy Thursday vigil and of the morning of Good Friday when students at a rural boarding school are allowed to make visits before the exposed Blessed Sacrament in the Lady Chapel. Richard, the protagonist, has anticipated this vigil for months; and he has hoped to pray extremely well during his chapel visit. Yet his hopes are doomed; and the narrative is, in large part, a report of his failure, even though he does experience genuine religious emotion.

Richard wants to sustain his religious fervor, but his mind is constantly distracted throughout the hours portrayed as he attempts to pray. After leaving the chapel, he and two other boys disobediently decide to go for an early hour swim instead of reporting back to the dormitory. Their swim and the other actions of Richard during the outing are distractions from his valiant effort to be religious. These hours include moments of high religious emotion, with hints that they must inevitably pass. The beauty of Agee's portrayal combines the awareness of inevitable diminishment along with a genuine apex of religious feeling.

Some critics believe the ending is ineffective. Commentary often either expresses dissatisfaction with the lack of a clear development in Richard's character, or explains that development in terms of the rather obvious symbolism.[9] Agee's emphasis, however, seems to be much more simply upon the evocation of a particular fleeting moment than many readers expect. Attention to the particularities of what Richard sees and imagines is the primary means of evoking what he feels.[10] And, while what he experiences, both inside and outside the chapel, does alter consciousness, he feels at the end of his Good Friday's experience that he and his schoolmates remain "children."[11]

As Agee planned this book, he noted that his focus was to be on religious emotion mixed with the "beginning of intrusions of [a] sense of beauty and a sense of science," while the general "watershed" about which the story was to flow was to remain the "age of faith at its height."[12] The boy's growing awareness about the complexity of his consciousness is the vehicle, but his desire to feel his faith, as well as other influences on that desire, is the core to which all events of *The Morning Watch* are related. The religious fervor of these hours essentially is bounded by other experiences, and ultimately these hours will be lost; but, during the watch, the emotion is relatively clear. Many forces at play within Richard's mind are almost balanced, but he is unaware of this. He is a rather bright twelve year old attempting to feel religious.

Holy Weeks in this story were special times for everyone, a time so special that even Willard Rivenburg, the "great athlete" of the school (who never even bothered to cross himself at crucial times in football games) was affected by the "stillness" which "came over everything" (21). For Richard, the events of that week were the culmination of an elaborate series of attempts to foster religious emotion. As Maundy Thursday arrives, he is near an apex in religious feeling. During the entire year preceding Holy Week, Richard had, he thought, elaborately intensified his fervor. Denial and mortification had been practiced throughout that year and even more so during the forty days of Lent. Just as his initial thoughts about the importance of his approaching watch are interrupted while still in bed, his attempt to cultivate religious emotion is doomed to continual distraction.

As the narrative opens, Richard lies awake waiting to be called to go to the chapel. He tries to meditate about Christ's Passion. But these attempts are broken by the happiness and blasphemy of other boys in the dormitory and by his own intellectual distractions. Occasionally in prayer he had been able to imagine Christ crucified; but often, as is the case when he is walking out of the dormitory, the image he imagined "was very little different from a pious painting" (11).

The attempt to pray in the chapel continues the pattern of distraction. As Richard kneels, he recalls the enormous lengths to which his self-imposed acts of mortification had been carried. It does not seem possible for Richard to have gone further than eating worms and nearly tasting his excrement (44). And indeed, he cannot. His self-imposed program of penance and mortification becomes confused in his mind with imaginary acts that he might perform, and his mind runs riot. He imagines himself crucified—a Tennessee news item; a newspaper headline flashes to mind: "STRANGE RITES AT MOUNTAIN SCHOOL." And suddenly he sinks "his face into his hands and prays in despair. 'O God forgive me!' " (51). Later, when he returns to the chapel for another half-hour watch he comes close to the realization for which he has been striving. Agee's working notes indicate that Richard's prayer would "finally, break through to sincere if over emotional realization." When he opens his eyes "in quiet wonder," it then seems "to him the very day. Not just a day in remembrance, but the day" (86).

But, when that height of religious emotion is felt, it is also made clear it will diminish. Richard realizes that on this day Christ will not see the sun set, and then he notices almost simultaneously, the candles on the altar "spearing, aspiring, among the dying flowers" (86). His realization of Good Friday is lost, and an emotion, vaguely unsettling, takes hold:

Something troubled him which he had done or had left undone, some failure of the soul or default of the heart which he could not now quite remember or was it perhaps foresee; he was empty and idle, in some way he had failed. Yet he was also filled to overflowing with a reverent and marveling peace and thankfulness. My cup runneth over, something whispered within him, yet what he saw in his mind's eye was a dry Chalice, an empty Grail (87).

Only in years following will Richard be able to realize that his active imagination coupled with religious fervor (not religious emotion alone) kindled the image of a "dry Chalice." With that image Agee hints at what is in store for Richard in the years after this high point of emotion fades.

Much of the section of the book devoted to his attempts to pray is a record of a distracted mental state, a constant series of deviations from the path Richard desperately wants to follow. For instance, he is hardly in the chapel when its atmosphere of candles and flowers, which should allow him to think of God, drives his mind to remembrances of his father's funeral. When he tries to pray "Soul of Christ sanctify me . . . Blood of Christ inebriate me," his thoughts immediately flash to his interest in the derivation of the word "inebriate"; and it is not long before he recalls "drinking soda pop in Knoxville [with] boys slightly more worldly than he [who] would twist the bottle deep into the mouth and cock it up vertically to drink . . . 'Ahhh, good ole whiskey!' " (33). But the "Blood of Christ" was not whiskey, he thought. Blood. And then, all of the sudden, he recalled blasphemous remarks which his uncle had made, " 'There is a pudding filled with blood.' " Finally, when

Richard forces such thoughts out of his mind momentarily, the word "Wounds" does the same thing.

The same pattern of distraction continues throughout the watch. Even when he realizes how he is sinfully distracted, he immediately sees that he is proud, and that, too, is sinful: "it began to occur to him that not many people would even know . . . the terrible sin it was" (78). Richard is balancing on a precarious ledge. When he recognizes his offense, he immediately seeks to balance it with resolution "until it began to seem as if he were tempted into eternal wrong by rightness itself or even the mere desire for rightness and as if he were trapped between them, good and evil, as if they were mirrors laid face to face . . ." (78–79). Richard wants desperately to maintain what he assumes to be a proper frame of mind, but Agee knew that the hours of devotion before the monstrance represented only a high point for Richard.

The working notes and the excluded manuscript, written in conjunction with the novella, support a reading which emphasizes the futility of the protagonist's attempt to sustain his simple faith as it is intruded upon by all manner of things from sex to skepticism. In these notes Agee asked himself what he hoped to accomplish;[13] and his answers, as well as an unused introductory and concluding passage, indicate that he felt the story should imply that innocence would yield to other ways of experiencing the world. Agee asked himself the following:

> What really am I after in this story, and is it worth doing? Religion at its deepest intensity or clarity of childhood faith and emotions; plus beginnings of a skeptical intellect and set of senses; how the senses themselves, and sexuality, feed the skeptical or non-religious or esthetic intellect; efforts at self-discipline. Religious-esthetic-biological experiences carrying with them above all, religious experience of an unusually fine kind, and the innocent certainty that it is doomed.

When, for instance, Agee suggests Richard's attempts to feel religious are clouded by his remembrances of pious paintings, he implies for the reader that the young artist-to-be is distracted by a developing aesthetic sense. The phrase "Within Thy wounds hide me" gives rise to a series of distractions, until finally "in his mind's eye, made all the worse by all the most insipid and effeminate, simpering faces of Jesus that he had ever seen in pictures, was this hideous image of a huge torn bleeding gulf at the supine crotch, into which an ant-swarm of the pious, millions of them . . . struggled to crowd themselves." Agee noted that he wanted to do the book in terms of "the watching in the chapel; wanderings of the mind and efforts at prayer; memories of the dead father; imaginations of sex and sport; workings of guilt; excesses of religious intention and complications of guilt and pride; the excitement of . . . dawn . . . the locust hull; . . . the snake." But he then asked:

Is [the snake] too obvious a symbol, and the locust? They seem so.

Is this worth doing? I can't get any solid hold of it or confidence in it.

A much gentler way of seeing and writing it? Or more casual? Mine is very dry and very literary.

His notes suggest reasons for little concern with characterization or plot in the book. He wanted to evoke "religious-esthetic-biological experiences." And he expresses doubt about his use of symbolism, the one element of the book most criticized. Richard Chase argues that, in place of "relaxed and perspicacious biography of spiritual change," the concluding parts of the book provide "spectacular semantic gestures."[14] If there is excessive symbolism within the concluding pages, however, that part of the narrative is small, in quantity and import, in comparison with the dominant second part about Richard's attempts at prayer. The basic concern in the central narrative and in the final section is an image of an intently religious boy during hours which encompass the most solemn religious feast of the year.

Agee realized that perhaps too many elements in his narrative were too elaborately developed. In another of his notes, he suggested that he was suspicious of "so many particularities. They drag, and they are dull. I keep working for the maximum number, an inch-by-inch account, when what I am after is the minimum in word and image, and a short handing of action."[15] For such reasons, he may have included the symbolism of the concluding section. For instance, the shell which Richard finds, and is fascinated with, certainly connotes death and suffering; but Agee was doubtful about the effectiveness of this symbol. Its function in the narrative suggests a change in the boy's awareness about suffering; and his awareness will, importantly, provide a propensity for later development. But, as the book closes, he does not fully understand what the locust shell signifies.

Similarly, after he kills the snake (Satanic, but also Christ-like), he realizes that his hand is fouled. He vaguely senses an equation between his brave action and his religiosity.

> He looked coldly at his trembling hand: bloody at the knuckles and laced with slime . . . .
> "Better warsh that stuff off," Hobe said. "Git in your blood; *boy!*"
> . . . he began to feel that he had been brave in a way that he had never been brave before and he wanted the hand to clear gradually and naturally, the way the smudge clears from the forehead on Ash Wednesday. (111)

Richard senses that all things fade; but, at this moment, he cannot fully realize that his religious emotion, which he has been desperately trying to enflame, will also fade. Almost immediately the boys go back to their dormitory; and, as they are walking, Richard remembers with "surprise and shame" what day it is and then thinks more about the Passion.

Several crucial events occur to Richard in the last episode of the book which prepare him for his later and inevitable change, even though he does not mature during these few hours. What he does experience provides him with knowledge for later change. More is expected of Richard than Agee hoped to handle, or could in a work of this scope, if readers expect the protagonist to exhibit a change in character.

Religiosity, yet simultaneously intense religious emotion, support Richard's actions throughout the book. After he leaves the Lady Chapel, his physical experiences become more important, but the effect of the change is not something about which he is fully aware. The air outside the chapel is "so different from the striving candles and the expiring flowers that the boys were stopped flat-footed on the gravel" (91); but Richard does continue to remind himself that it is Good Friday.

When F. W. Dupee initially reviewed the novella, he noted that its final scene at the Sand Cut was "not so well conceived" as the section set in the chapel; and he wondered if the "triumph in the chapel is not being capitalized on to an extent that is hardly legitimate."[16] The focus in the novella, even during the forbidden swim, remains on Richard's religious fervor. In that climactic scene, the dive and the attempt to stay under water an extremely long time are acts of pride and crucial steps in Richard's maturation; but they also become acts of devotion. The dive is symbolic of a rebirth after failure to sustain the kind of emotion that he hoped for while in the chapel; for, as Richard dives, he has "just time to dedicate within himself *for Thee!*"; and as his lungs are about to burst, he prays "O Lord let me suffer with Thee this day" (104). The religious emotion itself is near bursting. Richard is still able, a moment later, to stand on the bank of the quarry and think of what Jesus had suffered.

The concluding section remains fundamentally built on a boy's intently religious attitudes during hours which remain very much part of a religious feast. Agee's fear that his method of writing was perhaps elaborate and too "literary" provides insight into his accomplishment—a sense of immediacy and an evocation of emotion, but an emotion almost ready to disintegrate. In a related note, Agee suggests that "R's waking emotion and the hollowness of the dormitory beds must be as nearly immediate and simultaneous as possible."[17] Any indirection, abstraction, or use of symbols, unless very carefully integrated into the experience as a whole, would tend to detract from the immediacy of that moment. No doubt Agee experienced difficulty in deciding how best to focus on Richard's emotion. Several draft versions exist for alternate openings for the book; and, in addition, an introductory section and alternate ending were actually typed. Whether these alternate passages were submitted to an editor is unknown.

The introductory manuscript is from the point of view of an adult. In the excluded passage, Father Whitman, the priest who wakes the boys in the opening pages, tries to feel but cannot the solemnity of the night. For him, the meaning of the Passion is clear intellectually but not emotionally. His disturbed thoughts provide an insight into Richard's dilemma: "I only want to be a religious, he told himself quietly. I haven't got it in me to be, and in twenty years of trying, none of that has changed." He then immediately strikes his breast: "and prayed for forgiveness if possible for his doubt of his avowed and long tested vocation, and for support in his faith and in his efforts to discharge his duties as best he might, whether or not his heart was ever for an instant rewarded." Then Father Whitman's mind is distracted by his pocketwatch: "When at last the watch marked sixteen minutes of four, he briefly and formulatically completed his prayers, made the long firm sign of the cross which usually for a little while deeply confirmed him in his faithfulness, shut off the alarm, got up from the cot, and went as silently as he could down the corridor into Number Twelve to wake three more boys."[18] The implication of Richard's growing awareness, qualified by the opening description of Father Whitman, is that, with maturity, religious emotion becomes complicated by intellect and is easily distracted. Throughout the novella, Richard is not particularly aware of what he is experiencing; but he senses the difficulty of what he tries to accomplish. He cannot yet understand that religious emotion will not be forced.[19] In the excluded passage, the dull emotion of Father Whitman stands in contrast with the "sincerely devout" feelings of Richard.[20] Father Whitman, who has been a member of his Order for twenty years, tries to meditate.

In conjunction with the unused introductory passage, the "possible addition" for the conclusion would also have slightly altered the book's emphasis. That passage was written for the same purpose as the introductory passage. Agee suggested that if the alternate opening were employed, lines would "be added onto present ending, no new paragraph." The additional words were added onto the working draft.

On the last page of the narrative Richard approaches the dormitory with his errant friends; he is carrying the locust shell which he had picked up in the woods, "his left hand sustaining, in exquisite protectiveness, the bodiless shell which rested against his heart" (120). The excluded ending would have added these phrases: ". . . and exactly as he had foreseen, there on the back steps was Father Whitman, and although his eyes too were just as Richard had foreseen, hard, sleepless, patient, eyes to be afraid of and ashamed before, it was not so very hard to meet them after all."

Had Agee chosen to include both excluded sections of his manuscript, the design of his book would have been more apparent. With a beginning which suggests the difficulty of sustaining religious fervor and a conclusion which again returns to Father Whitman, the emphasis upon an "age of faith at its height," but doomed to collapse, would have been more clearly evident.

Throughout *The Morning Watch*, Agee is primarily concerned with suggesting the complex emotion of a particular imagined moment, a high point in Richard's life. Agee is fascinated with the beauty of that moment and with the reality of Richard's emotion.

Its beauty is mostly in its immediacy, and not so much in implications. Richard continues to force religious emotion up to the last moments of the book; when he tries least, he comes closest to genuine religious feeling. He is not aware of the vast differences between what he has attempted to experience during these hours and what actually has happened. Such a realization can only be made by a wiser person: Father Whitman or the artist.

Throughout his fiction Agee was interested in precisely focusing upon the intersections of space, time, and consciousness, and less so in constructing plots or in developing character. *The Morning Watch* at times resembles *Let Us Now Praise Famous Men* in which the writer concentrates upon particularities which are often complex states of mind. This semiautobiographical novella recalls the atmosphere of St. Andrew's, the boarding school near Sewanee, Tennessee, remembered by Agee from childhood; and real persons are surely the basis for much of its characterization. In the working notes a list of remembered names parallels a list of characters.[21] One must assume that real events had some bearing on the inception of the story.

Ohlin has suggested Richard's gradual change in awareness about suffering and death is the theme of the book.[22] This element is important; but equally important is the almost static quality of the imagined hours. The futility of Richard's effort to prolong a doomed emotion is at the core. The artist looks back upon his own precocious childhood, a time during which a twelve-year-old boy could hardly have perceived the complexity of what he was experiencing.[23]

Agee knew that religious emotion, for any person, was a combination of many different elements conjoined; but, as one matures, religious feeling is difficult to reconcile with other ways of feeling and thinking. For him, the late 1940s had been a time of religious questioning, as his letters to Father Flye in 1948 reflect. Several times he noted his feelings were cyclical "between feeling relatively uninvolved religiously and very much" so. Sometimes he felt a return to formal religion might be necessary for him, while at other times he was sure he would never return. But, along with these vacillations, he could say "at all times I feel sure that my own shapeless personal religious sense . . . is deepening and increasing."[24] Whether or not he might ever again have been a formal believer, his interest in religion remained important; for one of his letters of that period says simply "I certainly feel no doubt to which side I am drawn 'as between Christ and those against Him.' "[25]

Another fact which contributed to Agee's religious awareness during the late 1940s was his return to the campus of St. Andrew's during the early months of 1949 when he went to be present at the bedside of his dying stepfather. Spending a few days on the campus where he had spent five years must have moved his mind imaginatively to the time when religious belief and ritual had been more important. Still another indication of an interest in religious matters preceding the composition of this novella is Agee's contribution as an "amateur" to a *Partisan Review* symposium "Religion and the Intellectuals." In it, Agee reiterated that he veered "between belief in God, nonbelief, and a kind of neutrality. In all three frames of mind I keep what I believe is meant by the religious consciousness."[26] He stressed that religious belief, and conversion, is something ultimately inexplicable by rational means alone. "Certainly the final difficulty, for the intellectual only a little more so than for others, is that the crucial gap between religious belief and non-belief cannot be closed—still less kept closed—rationally."

Agee had been seriously thinking about religious questions during the years immediately preceding his decision to write *The Morning Watch*. The book appears to have been mostly written with a single spurt of energy during the spring of 1950.[27] Agee had spent "most of winter and spring" on an essay about John Huston, and then in one week a draft for the MaundyThursday story was finished. The book is, therefore, the product of a period preceded by religious awareness, and work which was written with relative speed, and is an attempt artistically to recreate an earlier time of felt emotion.

CHAPTER 9

Remembrances of Childhood

I *Plans for A Novel*

J UST as *Famous Men* expresses the reality of what had been
observed in middle Alabama and just as *The Morning Watch*
relies heavily upon autobiographical remembrance, Agee's final
book, unfinished at his death, is largely based on fact: he consciously sought to reconstruct the setting of his childhood. If *Famous Men*
is a memorial to tenant farmers, *A Death in the Family* is a
memorial for the writer's family—and especially for his father.
Agee's novel was not limited to accounts of father and son; the entire atmosphere sustained by events and persons remembered
became material for the fictionalized remembrance. In one of the
working notes for the book, Agee indicated that the days and
months preceding the fictional death were as significant as those
immediately surrounding the funeral.

As a tentative outline he sketched this pattern: "Begin with complete security and the simple pleasures and sensations. Develop: the
deficiency in the child which puts them at odds: the increasing need
of the child for the father's approval. Interrupt with the father's
sudden death. Here either the whole family is involved, or it is told
in terms of the child. At end: the child is in a sense and degree
doomed, to religion and the middle class. The mother to religiosity.
New strains develop . . . . ."[1] He made several similar listings of
possible episodes, and the evidence suggests that Agee, at least early in the composition, had in mind a considerably longer work than
the one we know as *A Death in the Family*. Had he lived to complete his book, or had he been able to continue in the natural direction which his remembrances were leading, he might have
amplified the atmosphere of family life preceding the death of his
father; for most of the variant manuscript material is from Rufus's
point of view.

The composite working draft for *A Death in the Family* consists of 194 handwritten manuscript pages, and an additional 114 pages of variant. Of the variant manuscript, twenty-three pages consist of notes and summary of action. The composite draft was carefully followed in the preparation of the book, but some significant manuscript was not incorporated. Such omission usually occurred only where a more detailed version was inserted. A close textual study of the entire autograph manuscript also reveals minor errors in transcription of Agee's minute pencil script.[2] Most relevant to an understanding of the novel are the notes and variants which accompany the working draft and which were apparently composed during an early stage. But Agee's methods for uniting different episodes which have no place in the primary time sequence remain unclear.[3] He may have intended to place this "interchapter" material at the beginning of the book without any connections between passages, for he had planned additional revision. Accompanying listings of additional possible episodes are notes which concern Rufus's doing "badly at the corner," that is, in his encounters with other boys. Agee notes that "possibly" he "should bring the corner conflict into sharper connection with the sudden death."[4] Within the composite novel in two episodes Rufus meets boys at the corner, but whether or not the additional material might have been developed about Rufus's teasing remains unknown. It is unfortunate that more episodes from Rufus's point of view are not complete, and the presence of manuscript fragments which emphasize the child's experience before his father's death emphasizes the type of episodes Agee might have developed at greater length.

Apparently Agee began writing the novel with its emphasis upon the relationship between Rufus and Jay. Thus, in a note labeled "Maximum simple, " he commented that the novel would ideally be "just the story of my relation with my father and, through that, as thorough as possible an image of him: winding into other things on the way but never dwelling on them."[5] The composite novel is clearly different from that intention, for the presentation of the death and funeral are predominant. Nevertheless, remembrances of moments distinct from the days which surrounded the funeral are a basic part of the book. Since the editors recognized the natural tripartite division of the composite novel (before Jay's death; the

waiting; and the funeral), the placement of the nonsequential interchapter material between the natural divisions of the story was
logical. But the italicized sections are as essential to the final effect
as the main narrative.[6] All of the variants written for A Death
should eventually be made available.

The novel, posthumously published in 1957, was well received by
reviewers, and has subsequently become well known. Many
reviewers were quick to observe that it was not really a novel but
"brilliant narrative and lyric fragments given editorially the
semblance of a novel."[7] Chapters 1 through 20, the narrative of
death and funeral, do form a complete unit; and they certainly
function as a novel. Because the italicized sections fall outside the
main narrative, comparing the work with other novels is difficult.
As Alfred Kazin notes, "it is an utterly individual and original
book" which does not follow expected patterns.[8]

The main narrative of A Death is about an evening's walk to the
movies, a call early in the morning which sends Jay ironically to his
own sick father's bedside, and the subsequent waiting for news
about Jay after his accident. These events are balanced by the confrontation with the reality of his death, preparations for the burial,
and the details of the funeral. But such bare summary gives hardly
any indication of how the book functions because the book is about
life, not death. Insights are provided section by section into the
minds of family members as they accept the knowledge of Jay's
death, and the novel is structured so that different episodes show
each family member's reaction to the news. That news, essentially
bewildering, allows Agee to focus on the separate values of Mary,
Aunt Hannah, her parents, and others.[9] The focus is provided
primarily by a careful observation of detail and rhythm.[10] The result
is almost as if Agee begins over and over to tell the same story from
slightly different angles.

The patterning of chapters in A Death is carefully balanced. The
first and the last are statement and counterstatement; the fifth
chapter, in which the children are first introduced together, and the
sixth chapter, in which Ralph acts like a child, support each other.[11]
Most importantly, the book begins with an opening episode which
clearly delineates the strength of the marriage and family and
which contrasts with the closing chapters, in which Mary's only
strength seems to come from her religion. Other elements which

contribute to the structural unity of the book are recurrent motifs—references to country people, darkness, even the tiles of the kitchen floor. (Jay muses: Mary was correct: A more subdued pattern would have been better.) Such motifs unify the book and remind the reader of the differences in attitude brought about by Jay's country background and the urban setting of the family's life. When Jay is driving to his father's bedside, the country ferryman seems to function allegorically, as if Jay is being delivered from the alien city.

Because of such emphasis, the interchapter material contributes to a full understanding of the novel. Those sections when Rufus is teased, either by his Uncle Ted or by boys in the neighborhood, or when he is shown at ease with his parents, clarify his relationship to his family, and imply some of what will be lost with the father's death. The section in which Jay comforts Rufus by singing is the most obvious of this group; Jay's ability to comfort is implied elsewhere. In the darkness chapter, he reassures Rufus; then he sings; but he is reminded during the singing of his own childhood and of his mortality. Jay begins to remember his mother's comforting him when he was a child. He could almost hear his mother or her father "and they in their childhood under other hands, away on back through the mountains, away on back through the years" (94).[12] Each of the italicized chapters functions like the meditative passages of *Let Us Now Praise Famous Men* and provides insight into the mystery of family life.

Agee's story, while simple on the surface, confronts death as the negation of life, but as a necessary part of it. The book provides an image of life which contrasts with the change brought about by sudden death, and commentators have described the book as the fulfillment of a vision where innocence and compassion meet.[13] In the composite novel, from its opening where Rufus feels enclosed by his father's laughter, to the closing moments when he is alone with his uncle, the focus remains on domestic love and family relationships. But, while *A Death in The Family* remains a private book, it is also about all who have undergone similar experiences; for Agee was aware that what he fictionalized possessed archetypal meaning.[14] What he experienced growing up in a comfortable neighborhood in a relatively small city with parents who shared urban and rural traits resembled the lives of thousands.

His fictional method is an extension of his continuing interest in documentation: everything remembered became potentially useful. A great respect for the commonplace is at the base of what is accomplished; and remembrances take on significance simply because they contributed to a previous atmosphere.[15] The word "poetic" often occurs in descriptions of the novel; and many perceptive insights about its form derive from the realization that *A Death in The Family* is more like a poem than a novel. Its open form provides a tension between the chaos of reality and the poet's way of writing about it.[16] Through careful attention to ordinary aspects of human experience, Agee reveals larger meaning. Dwight Macdonald observes, for instance, that "the nuances of the husband-and-wife relationship come out in a series of everyday actions . . . peppering the eggs . . . straightening the covers."[17] Such detail draws poetry from everyday observations.

II   *The "Dream Sequence"*

A Death in the Family is primarily concerned with evoking earlier moments from Agee's life. As he grew older, he was increasingly aware of the significance that he had become a certain person, under his mother's influence, and in the absence of a father whom he associated with a rural background. In the novel, the religion (and religiosity) of the fictional mother becomes a basic ingredient in her reaction to the death of her husband. The fictional parents experienced tension in their marriage, "a gulf," the mother thought, which had only recently begun to close; but their marriage grew into a strong bond beneficial to all of the family members. The father's death abruptly breaks that bond, and the more genteel qualities of the mother become dominant. Her reliance upon church, symbolized by Father Jackson, contrasts with earlier parts of the book when the true father is present. Father Jackson, as a strict interpreter of religious law, decides that Jay cannot be given the entire burial service because he had not been a formal church member—a strictness that contrasts with the easy-going strength of Jay who is appealing precisely because he is independently strong. The inference is that Rufus will become more reliant upon organized religion after his father's death and that the naturalness and openness of the father will be missed and become only something to imagine later.

Agee had wanted to write about his father's death as early as age sixteen, and some of his best writing accomplished during the 1930s relies on his remembrance of family.[18] His 1936 sketch "Knoxville: Summer of 1915," chosen by his editor, David McDowell, as a prelude to *A Death in the Family*, is a short sketch, written at least a decade before the book was begun, that evokes the peaceful atmosphere Rufus and his family enjoy. However, recollection of that peacefulness alone is not the mood which generated the novel. In "Knoxville: Summer of 1915" a time of unison with nature is recalled, as a city's noises are blended with natural ones. The mood which generated the novel is more evident from an excluded fragment now called "Dream Sequence." Edited since the novel's publication, this manuscript suggests that, through the work of art, a harmony with the past can be achieved; but the artist must first exorcise the nightmare of contemporary life before the peacefulness of *A Death in the Family* can be created.

"Dream Sequence," which begins in a nightmare, may have been intended as an introduction for the novel.[19] It evokes the state of mind of an author driven to compose an autobiographical novel so that artistic order can be made from memories related to the present. "Dream Sequence" has a completely different tone from the "Knoxville: Summer, 1915" sketch; however, both passages raise similar questions about identity and the mystery of being a person. In the "Dream," Agee states that he must return to the years of his childhood; in "Knoxville," he has already accomplished exactly that on a minor scale. "Knoxville" evokes the atmosphere of evenings enjoyed in childhood, and the remembrance of such moments is the core of Agee's lyrical writing at "his self-forgetful best."[20] In the "Dream," he explicitly acknowledges that memories from earlier experience retain a distinct beauty which can be evoked; and, when such evocation is successful, meaning is projected into the chaos and mystery of living.

In the "Dream Sequence," a personal remembrance, images from childhood are fused with the horror of contemporary times. In its nearly surrealistic method, the passage differs from all of Agee's other writing and resembles the technique of Céline.[21] The way a scene can suddenly shift from broiling heat to freezing cold, or the maddening way people on a street ignore the horrible, is reminiscent of *Journey to the End of the Night*. As Agee's "Dream" is read,

it becomes clear that only the individual act of integrity has meaning. The phraseology of "Dream," especially in the beginning, is
much like that of the "1928 Story," and the same disappointment
with the contemporary world pervades each. Elements from the
present are fused with facts about childhood when the death, the
absence, and the "betrayal" of the father are related to disappointments of the dreamer with his contemporary world. But it is
impossible to understand fully how past and present are related, for
what is significant is that after the nightmare has been suffered, the
dreamer knows he should "go back" into earlier years.

Frustration is reflected in Agee's postwar writing, and his disappointment with his failure to write often kept him from writing at
all. Such a listless mood is described in "1928 Story," and in unpublished poetry which reflects a longing for the clarity and beauty
of earlier times. In his "Dream," the explicit point is made that
something resembling the clarity of earlier times can be achieved by
the artist. As Agee began this book, his focus was to be limited only
to what he could recall: "nothing except (so well as he could
remember) what his father had been as he had known him, and
what he had been as he had known himself, and what he had seen
with his own eyes, and supposed with his own mind." In a related
manuscript note he wrote, after listing possible material from
Rufus's point of view, "No, these things wd [sic] be unconnected in
his experience & so here." With evidence from such notes and the
"Dream Sequence," it seems that, in an important sense, this was
not to be a novel of one organic unit with all its episodes woven
together.

Although Agee wanted to write about his relationship with his
father, his knowledge of it was fragmented; and for that reason the
presentation would be partial and would depend upon the recreation of portions of childhood to achieve an answer. "Nothing he
could hope to understand out of [the dream] was not already obvious to him. All the same, he could make the journey, as he had
dreamed the dream, for its own sake without trying to interpret;
and if the journey was made with sufficient courage and care, very
likely that of itself would be as near the answer as he would ever
hope to get."

A basic theme of A Death in the Family is the need for security,
the impossible desire to feel at home, seen in the opening chapters

as Jay and Rufus walk from the movie. The same motif appears in the "darkness" chapter; and the longer manuscript version of that chapter is more detailed because Jay remembers his own childhood and muses about his inability to return to earlier times. This motif is connected with Jay's ironic journey which leads to his accidental death and with the family's trip to LaFollette. Rufus's desire for approval and the mother's reliance on religion also demonstrate a similar need. The desire for security is again reiterated at the closing of the book when Rufus walks with his Uncle Andrew. The "Dream Sequence" symbolizes Agee's realization that he had to transcend the horror of the contemporary world—even his own confusion—if he were to create fiction which reflected earlier times. If the artist stops trying to make sense of the world and just responds to its mystery, it becomes possible to celebrate existence. In that way one does return home.

III   *Nostalgia and Honor for the Past*

The closing tone of "Dream Sequence" is similar in its mood to the first chapter of Agee's novel, and both evoke a peacefulness made possible when father and son are together. The opening chapter recounts a typical evening when Rufus and Jay had gone to the movies and had walked home. A basic idea in the book is fundamental to this episode—the insistence that, while one cannot be comfortable with the responsibilities of living, it is necessary to accept such frustration. Agee's stress on different characters' acceptance when frustrated is the most important single thematic element in this novel. Jay clearly does not feel completely at ease as a family man who lives in the city—with all the corresponding responsibilities—but he accepts this difficulty. After the Charlie Chaplin and William S. Hart movies are enjoyed, Rufus and his father begin walking home; but they stop, as they often did, at a saloon for a drink. They are barely through the door before Jay is looking up and down at faces to see if anyone is present from his home area, the Powell River Valley. During the rest of the walk home, no words are necessary for Rufus to sense that his father is uneasy. At such times the father and son often sat for a few moments on a limestone outcropping to enjoy the quiet. The need for solitude implies that Jay is not particularly happy; but the implication is that he and Rufus are learning how to accommodate themselves to dissatisfaction. After their separation by the abrupt death, such an influence is no longer possible for Rufus.

Agee emphasizes that in living there is no real security, for living leads inevitably to death. Contentment is fleeting, an illusion. But individual moments of love and domestic interchange nevertheless make it possible for individuals to bear living. Sometimes Agee's narrative borders on the sentimental, as is the case when Mary's parents are sitting together awaiting news about their son-in-law's accident. Joel almost reaches over to embrace his wife, but he cannot bring himself to do so. But his thought, this almost gesture, allows Agee to imply that love makes it possible not only to live day by day with disappointment but also to confront death. Human love sustains individuals. Even Rufus senses the discontentment of his father, who although he loved his family, "was more lonely than the contentment of . . . family could help" (19).

All of the characters in this novel are alone. As Agee focuses on them, especially as they react to the death, that loneliness is emphasized. But, ironically, circumstances surrounding the death allow individuals to be temporarily drawn together. Women characters are drawn together because of faith. The men, Uncle Andrew and the grandfather, react in anger, contempt, and pessimism; nevertheless, they, too, are momentarily drawn together. The accident of the death and circumstances of the moment allow individual acts of compassion.[22] The scene where the family gathers to await the news about Jay exemplifies how each individual can be drawn out of loneliness because of the needs of others. Mary's father, even though he is the skeptic of the family, does comfort his daughter.

A similar achievement is gained by the shifting point of view within the main narrative, which allows Agee to avoid dependence on any single character. Thus he can more easily celebrate the world imagined. When, for instance, Hannah and Mary await news about Jay, Agee provides information through both of their minds. After the family learns of Jay's death, Hannah, Mary, and Andrew meditate about the meaning of death.

Often sequences which celebrate experience are focused through Rufus's point of view—when, for instance, he goes shopping with Hannah and "the whole merchant world [is held] in a focus of delight" (75). The best sustained example of Rufus's sense of an atmosphere is found in the opening chapter when father and son are together. Its immediacy derives from the scrupulously careful attention Agee pays to real details as they flow before Rufus's and his father's eyes. The paragraph which relates how son and father enjoyed their movie has a rhythm which suggests the changing images of the screen. One paragraph is connected with a long series of "ands" and "thens," and its effect is almost a panoramic presentation of what Rufus and Jay see. Agee's decision to employ such a technique is the result of his conviction that the atmosphere which had been experienced during such evenings eluded complete verbalization. Thus, he concentrates upon the physical reality which helps to create a particular atmosphere. The wonder of the movie and the enjoyment father and son experienced watching it are the central concern, but how they felt during such a moment cannot be explained, and there has to be a substitution—a celebration of the physical reality which helped to make the emotion possible.

The same kind of situation occurs when Rufus sits with his father at their corner. Agee describes the comfort Rufus felt during those moments: "Rufus' father took off his hat . . . put it over the [point] of his bent knee. . . . Rufus felt his father's hand settle, without groping or clumsiness, on the top of his bare head . . ." (21). And during those moments the child felt "a particular contentment, unlike any other that he knew. He did not know what this was, in words or ideas, or what the reason was; it was simply all that he saw and felt" (19). The recorded physical details suggest the emotion; the careful record evokes the moment imagined.

A similar process is used for other episodes. The moods of the children listening to the sound of Father Jackson's voice as he attempts to comfort their mother or their viewing the dead father are suggested through careful attention to the physical scene. Agee shows characters learning to live with the fact of death, but he does not attempt to provide a resolution for the dilemma he charts. At the end of the novel, as Rufus walks with his Uncle Andrew, he becomes quite confused. He cannot understand why his uncle is so unhappy about the details of the burial, and his anger seems to occur for no reason. When Agee writes about the children listening to the muffled sounds of Father Jackson's comforting their mother on the morning of the funeral, he similarly uses that single event to convey the mood of the entire morning. It was not something which Rufus and Catherine could "understand"; but, because of the care with which details are described, the atmosphere is caught, an atmosphere of comfort and fright, of hope and fear. Such tension, made up of a complexity of emotion, is important throughout the novel.

Each of the events about which Agee chose to write is specific, but they suggest an atmosphere which is impossible to verbalize completely. The suggestion of such an atmosphere occurs when Agee imagines Jay thinking or when Rufus feels comfortable in the presence of his parents. The same specificity occurs when Mary awaits news of Jay and confronts the fact of his absence. Agee describes the people by his focus on the events of their daily life, either before or during the days of the funeral.

What is reported provides other implications. This method of precise observation suggests much about Jay and Mary when they arise after he is called to his father's bedside. Through minute observations an atmosphere which surrounds them is suggested: the details of how food is cooked, beds made, cars cranked, even shirts tucked in—all such peculiarities become significant. After Jay receives the phone call about his father's illness and decides that he must leave in the night, his eating of breakfast is carefully outlined. He does not really want the food which Mary cooks for him, he would be happier to go to an all-night lunchroom, since he "had not been in one since Rufus was born" (29), but he agrees to eat. His actions, just like his train of thought as he dresses, reveal his feelings at that moment; and the reader learns what sort of man he is and what sort of marriage his is—he is determined to eat the big breakfast so that he will not offend Mary, who enjoys feeding him but who senses that he is only pretending hunger. Such details provide a perspective adequate for a vision of different forces in conjunction to form moments of domestic love. Agee's method focuses on scenes which symbolize an atmosphere of fleeting happiness.[23] When Mary learns that Jay has been in an accident and that a sickroom may be needed, Agee's description of her preparation of the room reveals much about her love for Jay. She methodically prepares for his return while remembering an earlier time when he had been ill and had joked with her. Agee's picture of Rufus's parents combines the best qualities of both, and they are especially apparent in the contrasting scenes in which Jay and Mary, separately, sing to Rufus. He realizes that Jay loved to sing the old country songs, and that, when his mother tried to sound like a country singer, she could not do it. Her clear voice was not made for country songs. Rufus "liked both ways very much and best of all

when they sang together and he was there with them . . ."
(99–100). A similar blending of influence is suggested during a Sunday's trip to visit Jay's great-great-grandmother. On the way, both
parents attempt to determine how old the grandmother might be,
and Mary comments " '—*why she's almost as old as the country,
Jay.*' " Jay laughs:

"*Oh, no,*" . . . "*Ain't nobody* that *old. Why I read somewhere that just
these mountains here are the oldest* . . ."
"*Dear, I meant the nation,*" she said. "*The United States, I mean. . . .*"
(232)

Jay is thinking of the natural world, and she is thinking of the
organization of the government. Dealing in abstract concepts is not
his ordinary mode of thought; he deals much more immediately
with the concrete. Agee is not approving of Jay's or Mary's actions;
he simply documents the imagined result of an intricate blending of
attitudes. Relationships between family members are difficult to
suggest accurately in a work of fiction because of their ordinariness.
Agee's method catches the flavor of everyday family life. The interchapter about Mary's pregnancy is a further example of the
differences between the two parents who think and react to the
same set of circumstances. Jay is naturally direct, but not Mary. She
does not want to tell Rufus directly that they are going to have a
baby, and she is also indirect when she attempts to tell the children
that their father has been killed.

Agee lets each character find his way to a realization of the truth
by letting him talk, feel, and think within the immediacy of a particular situation. Aunt Hannah perhaps best realizes how this must
be done. Her care not to push Rufus into making a decision about
his cap and her restraint not to force ideas or opinions on Mary
while each awaits news from Andrew reflect Agee's own patience
with the fictionalization of a mystery. Hannah will let her niece
come to whatever realization she must, but on her own. At the same
time, Hannah comforts Mary as best she can, realizing that each
person is essentially alone.

Ultimately this book stands as a confrontation with the fact that
each person is alone. Agee presents many images of individuals, especially Rufus, piecing together the meaning of experiences that
finally cannot be understood, but only accepted. One of the most

appealing characteristics of Rufus and of his three-year-old sister is their trust. Their acceptance of life, which includes death, stands as an example for the adults who surround them.

What must be accepted is at the core of the narrative. Agee will not even condemn the drunken actions of Jay's brother, Ralph, although he pities him. Ralph apparently has lost the strength which sustains many other people. Walter Starr, who takes care of the children on the day of the funeral, also exemplifies Agee's emphasis on man's need for acceptance. Starr was instructed to take the children directly home after the funeral service at the grandparent's home, but he circles back so that they can see the casket being carried to the hearse since he feels they should see as much as possible. Earlier, Starr had decided to say something to the children about their father's being like Lincoln: "Not because you'll understand it now, but I have to, my heart's full . . . . Maybe you'll remember it later on" (302). He says that he often thought of Jay as being like Lincoln because both fought against extremely hard odds but were always honest in their endeavors. The reader infers that Starr's realization will have later significance for Rufus, while, within this fictional moment, Starr and the children are drawn together.

This novel suggests the problem *any* individual confronts by the mystery of living. Love, separation, compassion, innocence, comfort—these are themes constantly implied. When Rufus is wandering about the house on the morning after his father's death, his loneliness is conveyed by scrupulous attention to details observed. The child goes to his father's chair in the living room, smells it, feels it, and then he thinks of the ash tray: "it was empty. He ran his finger inside it; there was only a dim smudge of ash. There was nothing like enough to keep in his pocket or wrap up in a paper. He looked at his finger for a moment and licked it; his tongue tasted of darkness" (281).

Just as in the opening chapter, or at the burial service when the strong odor of flowers is observed, Agee's success derives from precise attention to sounds, images, and detail. Also, in descriptions of nature strategically placed throughout the book, he reminds the reader that the actions of men are finally infinitesimal when compared to the universe itself. As a book about domestic love, A *Death* treats the same subject as some of the undergraduate poems and the sonnet sequence of *Permit Me Voyage*. The difference is that this prose is removed from the conventions of poetic form and that particular memories suggest a mood.

The use of the devastated Fort Saunders as a setting for the final episode of the book demonstrates Agee's method and success. What better setting could be imagined to suggest a contrast between the shattered feelings at the closing and the mood predominant in the beginning? The Fort really existed as part of Agee's childhood neighborhood, and it becomes within the context of the book an excellent symbol for the impossibility of any man's being able to fortify his existence.

A novel about domestic love seems unpromising for a novelist in the middle part of the twentieth century. But delicate domestic love, experienced by millions, is what holds the remembrance together. Each action and gesture is unique; and, as these individual acts are performed, they have value within a unique framework. This realization prompted Agee to "go back into those years," and his "going back" was based upon a careful delineation of events which could be fictionally remembered or inferred. Because he so respected the real world as remembered, his novel was easily adapted into a drama and a film. The title of those adaptations is taken from the final sentence of the novel ". . . and *all the way home* they walked in silence." In the play and film, as well as the novel, one of the predominant facts which is experienced is the assurance that one is witnessing a passing way of life, suggested by the setting as well as the characterization. Yet, as one is reminded of inevitable change, it is possible to focus on a time when many forces were clearly in productive tension. Knoxville, Tennessee, at that time was small enough so that, after Jay's death, Mary's family could walk to her house; but the novel makes it clear that this was a city in which it was difficult to feel at home. Domestic tranquility exists, but it is fragile.

This novel is an evocation of remembrances of childhood. Because of the preciseness of its observations, Agee captures not just the image of his childhood, but a suggestion of what all families experience as they are buffeted by living.

CHAPTER 10

Accomplishment

"Soon you must wake, and dreams be done
When you behold the heavy sun."
[Unpublished poem]

I

COMMENTARY about the writing of James Agee often expresses the wish that the circumstances of his life could have been different, or that he could have had foresight to have written more poetry and fiction. But such futile speculation has little to do with what he paradoxically accomplished despite the frustrations which bounded his life. His career was partially formed by the Great Depression and World War II, and his entire generation might have developed differently under changed economic and social conditions. F. Scott Fitzgerald and Nathanael West also had careers which were shaped by the social conditions under which they worked; and Agee, like many of his contemporaries, was forced to adjust his sights to limited possibilities; but within these circumstances he developed into a notable writer who established himself in modern literature. "If it took him twenty years longer than it took Joyce," writes his editor Robert Fitzgerald, "who else arrived at all?"[1]

Had Agee been more disciplined or less ambitious, he might have written conventional volumes of poetry or short stories, or he might have even extended the reportorial writing begun with the Southern tenant experience; but he allowed himself to be distracted. He kept finding new things either to do, or to which he could react, and he was seldom bored by anything. His exuberance in conversation, his wit in correspondence, and his continual range of awareness evince how he was prevented from being a writer who did predictable things within a single category. Agee loved life as much as art, as his sustained interests in photography and music show. A more ruthless artist might have ignored other interests so that writing alone could have been cultivated, but Agee chose otherwise. For instance, for over a year during the late 1940s, when he might have been writing pages for *A Death in the Family*, he and Allen Tate played Beethoven and Mozart on piano and violin every Friday evening.[2]

Just as Agee might have been thought to be in some ways physically clumsy, the total production of his writing appears roughly hewn because he wrote in so many modes. This fact derives from his conviction that it is impossible to achieve a complete synthesis in life or art, but through art minimal order is imposed. His autobiographical writing and the tenant book imply that living is a dream for security which leads to death; but acceptance of life, which includes death, makes it possible to celebrate individual moments. In his writing, Agee reminds his readers that man is lost when he ceases to respect the fragility of his role in the universe. Throughout his career he was unhappy with the shoddy and the meretricious and impatient with modern culture when it fell short of its potential. For similar reasons, he was critical of himself when he evaluated his own writing. He was severe on himself and his contemporaries because he expected so much from both.

Agee distrusted much of the modern world's emphasis on science and rationalism, for he knew that there was more to life then could be explained or communicated through writing. At the same time, he was capable of spending years composing *Let Us Now Praise Famous Men*, while he knew that it was only a "dissonant prologue." He jokingly suggested that the best type of paper for *Famous Men* would be newsprint because in a hundred years it would deteriorate to nothing.[3] His best work grew out of such an awareness of man's limitations. His realization of man's finite capacity is at the center of his poetry and prose, and it allows him to celebrate individual moments.

Critics complain about Agee's unfulfilled promise because so much talent existed within a man who at each stage of a multifaceted career exploded with elaborate plans to write or to make films. He expected much of himself; and it has become possible to assume that more of his plans should have been brought to fruition, but to execute even his many projects for the criticism of popular culture would have taken a crew of Agees.[4] He was always distinctly alone. Nevertheless, while he was his own person, he never was isolated from society. His lamentations about the loss of individualism in America reveal much about his virtues and weaknesses. Less concern with individualism in the abstract might have profited him; but he was a man of enormous energy, and he sometimes mistakenly assumed that he had time and energy for everything.

II

In all of Agee's writing, there is an elegiac tone, for his are songs to moments which are passing. This nostalgia for the past and respect for the moment are his best achievements. His books are valuable because they are precise records of moments which are in process of passing away from memory. *Let Us Now Praise Famous Men*, *The Morning Watch*, and *A Death in the Family* each reflect particular moments Agee honored; his success is that he catches moments for others to appreciate.

Characteristic of Agee's vision is that, while realizing the transitoriness of all man's endeavors, he could pour all of his energy into a particular project at hand. Clear examples of this paradox are his draft lyrics for Lillian Hellman's *Candide*. His "culture song" shows what enjoyment can be had while emphasizing the impermanence of all "culture." In a variant, not included in *The Collected Poems*, the Governor cynically sings:

> Reason, Magic, Skill and, Love,
> Frankly, I think, poorly of.
> Flesh and Figment, Brain and Breath.
> All are parodies of Death.
>
> Death alone can paint it true;
> Only Death can say for sure;
> Who but Death can sing to you?
> Death my dearest, sparse and pure.
>
> Life is but a sorrowing haze
> Through which we grope; and our five senses,
> Trammeling snares. In all our way
> Artists put their subtle fences:

> Telling us that Life is All;
> Cheating us with hints of glory;
> Charming us. We fail, we fall
> Stupefied, and buy their story.[5]

To remember that such lyrics were written during the last years of Agee's life while he was aware of his own bad health is to be reminded of his consistent ability to confront the facts of living. These humorous lines reveal a fundamental ingredient in his use of the written word. Above all, he insisted that facts have a significance independent of any use which art might make of them. That insistence, as developed in *Let Us Now Praise Famous Men*, led him to a new way of documenting experience.

Famous Men is the keystone in Agee's career and there he made his most sustained contribution to American letters. His way of documenting what others had not even taken time to see is his most significant contribution to modern literature. His respect for the unsung beauty of common lives in rural Alabama is prophetic of a new kind of journalism, perhaps now best practiced by writers like Norman Mailer. Agee's importance in modern literature rests on his ability to write poetry and prose which go beyond traditional modes. Just as the poetry of *Permit Me Voyage* recovered the Elizabethan flavor of Agee's models but went beyond to reveal his own feeling, the book about sharecroppers went beyond any previous documentary produced in the 1930s. Agee's personal apprehension of actuality is always at the base of his writing. Thus he wrote in a manner reminiscent of Joyce in *The Morning Watch*, but the novella is about a crucial event in his memory, and the precision of *A Death in the Family* results from Agee's fictionalization of the ordinary.

Agee's concern with innocence and individualism amid the complexities of modern society is reflected in the similarity of theme in all of his literary writing, as well as in his screen adaptations. In each, he taught readers to see beauty in the commonplace and to be aware of man's frailty and innocence. As one might expect his influence is not just in literary areas. Robert Coles, who produced many studies of the deprived in America, has documented his reverence for Agee. Coles, active in the Civil Rights Movement, asserts that Agee's book was important for many during that crucial time when Americans learned to see what had not been properly seen before. Agee taught many how to perceive wholeness within an apparently drifting modern culture.

Much of his writing seems anti-institutional. Church, School, a publication like *Fortune* or *Time*, or even Hollywood have great potential for good. Often these institutions fall short of their capability because they are caught up with other matters which are ultimately degrading. Agee was a person often impatient with politics; yet he could seriously propose a new political party "based on the assumptions that people are most importantly themselves, not members of, or subjects to a government . . . ."[6] He was dissatisfied with the formal church, but some of his best writing catches the atmosphere which radiates from religious belief. Father Flye commented, "System of any kind was pretty irksome to him,"[7] but Agee knew that through man's institutions—fallible though they are—man performs. His was a quarrel with a world whose institutions had become tarnished.

When the Spring 1972 *Harvard Advocate* was dedicated to James Rufus Agee, its editor of forty years earlier, the students who paid him respect did special homage to the quality of his moral insights. The quality of that moral vision is a final reason why Agee's works have enduring value. He was a writer for whom there was little separation between moral and aesthetic judgments. There was never a question of anything being right if it did not honor the human spirit. He suspected any kind of construct which removed man from the immediacy of life ("kind, obscene philosophy" he sometimes said). But he knew that such frameworks were necessary if man were to be reminded of the immediacy of living and the continuity of life. The ultimate value of his poetry and prose is a celebration of immediacy bounded by death. In Agee's writing a continual celebration is of the ordinary facts of existence. A child's wonder, the pleasure to be gained from a chance encounter, the emotion of true religious faith—these are the kinds of things about which he wrote best. Always these are things which quickly pass, but through language they are arrested so that others can behold them.

Notes and References

Preface

1. *Letters of James Agee to Father Flye*, ed. James H. Flye, second edition (Boston, 1971), p. 153.
2. *Agee on Film*, (New York, 1967), I, 125.
3. Robert Fitzgerald, "A Memoir," in *The Collected Short Prose of James Agee* (Boston, 1968), p. 54.
4. Unpublished draft for an article: "For several years I reviewed movies for *Time* and for *The Nation*. . . ." Catalogued as [Piece for *New York Times*]. Autograph manuscript working draft with autograph emendations [14 pp.], University of Texas Library.
5. *Let Us Now Praise Famous Men* (Boston, 1941), p. 11.

Chapter One

1. Interview with Irvine Upham, San Antonio, Texas, August 10, 1966. Evans' comments are in his "James Agee in 1936," a foreword to the second edition of *Let Us Now Praise Famous Men* (Boston, 1960), pp. ix—xii.
2. Interview with David McDowell, Monteagle, Tenn., October 18, 1970.
3. P. M. Agee, *A Record of the Agee Family* (Independence, Missouri, 1937), p., 6.
4. Louise Davis, "He Tortured the Thing He Loved," *Nashville Tennessean Magazine*, February 15, 1959, p. 16.
5. Louise Davis, "Two Deaths in the Family," *Nashville Tennessean Magazine*, February 8, 1959, p. 11.
6. Commentary by Mrs. George McAfee, cited by Charles W. Mayo in his Ph.D. dissertation, "James Agee: His Literary Life and Work," (Peabody, 1969), p. 14; letter to Mayo by Dr. A. B. Tripp (April 13, 1968), p. 15.
7. Davis, "He Tortured the Thing He Loved," p. 15.
8. Commentary by John Stroup cited by Mayo, p. 18.
9. Robert Phelps, "James Agee," essay included in *Letters*, p. 7.

10. W. M. Frohock, "James Agee: The Question of Wasted Talent," *The Novel of Violence in America* (Dallas, 1957), p. 215.

11. Laura Tyler Wright, quoted by Louise Davis in "He Tortured the Thing He Loved," p. 15.

12. Letter to Dwight Macdonald, July 21, 1927.

13. Fitzgerald, "A Memoir," p. 6.

14. *Letters*, pp. 55—56.

15. *Ibid.*, p. 67.

16. *Ibid.*, p. 66.

17. *Ibid.*, p. 58.

18. Interview with Father James H. Flye, New York City, August 25, 1969.

19. *Letters*, pp. 68—69.

20. Evans, "James Agee in 1936," *op. cit.*, pp. ix—x.

21. "Before God and This Company; or Bigger Than We Are," Autograph manuscript, 5 pp., n.d., University of Texas Library.

22. "James Agee by Himself," *Esquire*, LX (December, 1963), 149 and 289. Paragraphs similar to this sketch accompany the variant manuscript for *Famous Men* now in the University of Texas Library.

23. Interview with David McDowell, Monteagle, Tenn., October 18, 1970.

24. *Famous Men*, p. 238.

25. *Agee on Film*, I, 33.

26. "They That Sow in Sorrow Shall Reap," *The Collected Short Prose of James Agee* (Boston, 1968), p. 85.

27. *Letters*, p. 47.

28. *Forum*, XCVI (February, 1937), 115—16.

Chapter Two

1. Interview with Father James H. Flye, New York City, December 28, 1966.

2. *Phillips Exeter Monthly*, XXX (March, 1926), 115—17.

3. *Ibid.*, XXX (December, 1925), 48—51; XXX (January, 1926), pp. 77—78.

4. *Ibid.*, XXXI (April, 1927), 161—66.

5. *Ibid.*, XXX (April, 1926), 143—51

6. *Ibid.*, XXX (November, 1925), 39—42.

7. *Ibid.*, XXXII (March, 1928), 133—37.

8. Jeanne M. Concannon, "The Poetry and Fiction of James Agee: A Critical Analysis," Ph.D. dissertation, (University of Minnesota, 1968), p. 101.

9. *Phillips Exeter Monthly* XXX (May, 1926), 167—71.

10. *Ibid.*, XXXII (November, 1927), 25—40.

11. *Ibid.*, XXXII (March, 1928), 133—37.

12. *Ibid.*, XXX (March, 1926), 122—26.

13. "Catched: A Play in Three Scenes," *Ibid.*, XXX (February, 1926), 87—97.

14. *Ibid.*, XXXI (June, 1927), 107—09.

15. *Ibid.*, XXXII (December, 1927), 59—65.

16. *Letters*, p. 37.

17. Concannon, *op. cit.*, p. 50.

18. *Phillips Exeter Monthly*, XXX (November, 1925), 27.

19. *Ibid.*, XXXII (May, 1928), 177—86.

20. "Pygmalion," Typed carbon copy manuscript, 4 pp., n.d., University of Texas Library.

21. See Alfred Barson's discussion of this poem in *A Way of Seeing*, A Critical Study of James Agee (Amherst, 1972), p. 24.

22. "Pygmalion" manuscript, *op. cit.*, p. 3.

23. All five of these poems have been reprinted in *The Collected Poems of James Agee* (Boston, 1968), p. 125, p. 126, p. 127. and p. 132.

24. *Collected Poems*, p. 129.

25. *Ibid.*, pp. 126—27.

26. *Ibid.*, p. 134.

27. *Ibid.*,

28. *Ibid.*, p. 133.

29. *Ibid.*

30. "A Parable of Doors," *Collected Poems*, p. 136.

31. "A Memoir," *op. cit.*, p. 11.

32. "A Walk Before Mass," *The Harvard Advocate*, CXVI (Christmas, 1929), 18—20.

33. *Collected Short Prose*, p. 74.

34. *Ibid.*, pp. 75—98.

35. *Collected Poems*, p. 28. This edition of *Permit Me Voyage* incorporates emendations which Agee made in a copy for Father Flye. All subsequent references to *Permit Me Voyage* are noted parenthetically.

36. Peter H. Ohlin, *Agee.* (New York, 1966), p. 31.

37. "Reflections on Permit Me Voyage," Typed manuscript, n.d., catalogued with "The Poems of James Agee and related documents," edited and with a memoir by Robert Fitzgerald, 1964, University of Texas Library.

38. Representative early reviews include the following: Horace Gregory, "The Beginning of Wisdom," *Poetry*, XLVI (April, 1935), 50; Lincoln Kirstein, "New Poems," *New Republic*, LXXXII (February 27, 1935), 80; and *Yale Review*, n.s. XXIV (Winter, 1935), p. 394.

39. Ohlin, p. 20.

40. *Collected Poems*, p. 128.

41. Ohlin, p. 41.

42. "Him We Killed and Laid Alone," *Collected Poems*, p. 56.

43. "Introduction" to *Collected Poems*, p.x.

44. J. Douglas Perry, Jr., "James Agee and the American Romantic Tradition," Ph.D. dissertation, (Temple University, 1968), p.37.

45. See Perry's explication, pp. 28—36.

46. See note 40.

47. Barson discusses the influence of Robinson Jeffers in *A Way of Seeing*, pp. 20—21.

48. "A Memoir," p. 7.

49. "Reflections on Permit Me Voyage," p. 1.

50. *Collected Poems*, pp. 53—55.

51. Concannon, p. 90.

52. This recording was made from tapes in the possession of Father Flye. "James Agee: A Portrait," Caedmon Records, 1971, TC 2042.

Chapter Three

1. *Collected Poems*, p. 151.

2. *Ibid.*, p. 144.

3. *Letters*, p. 67.

4. *Ibid.*, p. 82.

5. Dwight Macdonald, "A Way of Death," *Memoirs of a Revolutionist*, (New York, 1957), p. 262.

6. "The Great American Roadside," *Fortune*, X (September, 1934), 53.

7. "T.V.A.," *Fortune*, XI (May, 1935), 93—98, 140—53.

8. "August at Saratoga," *Fortune*, XII (August, 1935), 100.

9. "A Project for a poem in Byronics," *Collected Poems*, p. 79.

10. *Collected Poems*, p. 80. All subsequent references to "John Carter" are noted parenthetically.

11. *Collected Short Prose*, pp. 131—48.

12. *Ibid.*, p. 216.

13. "A Memoir," p. 50.

14. For a more detailed consideration of this screenplay consult Ohlin, p. 163; Barson, pp. 58—59, and Mayo, p. 147.

15. Ohlin, p. 163.

16. "A Memoir," p. 21.

17. *Collected Poems*, p. 155.

18. *Ibid.*, p. 153.

19. *Ibid.*, p. 148.

20. *Ibid.*, p. 155.

21. This poem was originally published as a prose poem. Fitzgerald prints it arranged as verse. *Collected Poems*, pp. 59—60.

22. Elizabeth Drew, *Poetry* (New York, 1959), p. 213.

23. *Collected Poems*, p. 165.

24. "Knoxville: Summer of 1915" originally appeared in the *Partisan Review*, V (August—September, 1938), pp. 22—25. The sketch is reprinted as a prologue in all editions of *A Death in the Family*.

25. *Collected Poems*, p. 71.

26. *Fortune*, XVI (September, 1937), p. 220.

27. Letter of Father Flye to James Agee, *Letters*, p. 248.

28. "Southeast of the Island: Travel Notes," *Collected Short Prose*, p. 177.

Chapter Four

1. *Letters*, p. 92.

2. *Ibid.*, p. 94. The recent study *Documentary Expression and Thirties America*, by William Stott (New York, 1973) illuminates the difference between Agee and Evans' book and other 1930s documentaries.

3. Autograph manuscript notebook, catalogued as "Let Us Now Praise Famous Men: Notes" [40 1.] n.d., University of Texas Library.

4. *Collected Short Prose*, p. 134.

5. Three exceptions who wrote favorably of Agee's text were Selden Rodman, *Saturday Review*, XXIV (August 23, 1941), 6; Lionel Trilling, *Kenyon Review*, IV (Winter, 1942), 99-102; and George M. O'Donnell, *Memphis Commercial Appeal*, section IV, September 7, 1941, 10.

6. John C. Cort, *Commonweal*, XXXIV (September 12, 1941), 499.

7. George Barker, *The Nation*, CLIII (September 27, 1941), 282.

8. Erik Wensberg, *The Nation*, CLXXII (November 26, 1960), 417.

9. Ohlin, p. 106.

10. Kenneth Seib, *James Agee: Promise and Fulfillment* (Pittsburg, 1968), p. 58.

11. Perry's dissertation is cited in note 44 of chapter 2; Barson's *A Way of Seeing, op. cit.*, is especially concerned with aesthetic parallels between Agee and Joyce. Stott's book is cited in note 2 of this chapter.

12. *Let Us Now Praise Famous Men* (Boston, 1941), p. 11. All subsequent references are noted parenthetically.

13. A partial carbon copy manuscript of *Famous Men* reveals that the complete "Part One" of the "Work" chapter is an elaborate attempt to suggest the reiterative qualities of all physical labor. See my edition of this material in the *Texas Quarterly*, XV (Spring, 1972), pp. 27—48.

14. *Letters*, pp. 104—05.

15. Commentators agree that Agee's text is highly structured: See Ohlin, pp. 61-107; and Perry pp. 83-130. Agee's own "Lyrics" [*Partisan Review*,

December, 1937] imply his realization of the difficulty of what he sought to write.

16. Note Agee's "Preamble," p. xv.

17. Agee's footnote: "The three sections of 'On the Porch' were written in 1937" (p. 244).

18. Compare Seib's interpretation of how the third plane functions, p. 48.

19. Ohlin, Perry, and Barson have independently demonstrated how aspects of the text contribute to its unification.

20. See note 13 of this chapter.

21. Wensberg, *op. cit.*, p. 418.

22. See William John Rewak, "The Shadow and the Butterfly, James Agee's Treatment of Death," Ph.D. dissertation, (University of Minnesota, 1970), p. 95 ff.

23. Agee uses the word "continuum" himself at p. 62.

24. Richard Hayes, "Rhetoric of Splendor," *Commonweal*, LXVII (September 12, 1958), 592.

25. Lionel Trilling, *Kenyon Review*, IV (Winter, 1942), 101.

26. Wensberg, *op. cit.*, p. 418.

27. Cort, *op. cit.*, p. 499.

28. Kenneth Burke, *Rhetoric of Motives* (New York, 1950), p. 146.

29. See my article, "Agee and Plans for the Criticism of Popular Culture," *Journal of Popular Culture*, V (Spring, 1972), 755–66.

30. My article "Agee's *Let Us Now Praise Famous Men:* Image of Tenant Life," *The Mississippi Quarterly*, XXV (Fall, 1972), 405–17, elaborates how Agee's text provides a picture of a way of life.

Chapter Five

1. Interview with Father James H. Flye, New York City, December 29, 1966.

2. Letter to Dwight Macdonald, June 16, 192 [7?].

3. *Letters*, p. 97.

4. *Time*, XXXV (February 19, 1940), 86.

5. *Letters*, p. 119.

6. Alfred T. Barson, "James Agee: A Study of Artistic Consciousness," Ph.D. dissertation, (Massachusetts, 1969), p. 77.

7. *Agee on Film*, I, 23–24. All subsequent references are noted parenthetically.

8. The notes for *A Way of Seeing* are catalogued as unidentified manuscript, working draft, n.d., University of Texas Library.

9. Ohlin, p. 125.

10. Autograph working draft with autograph emendations [25 pp.] [1947

Oct.], University of Texas Library.

11. See Perry, pp. 143—54, for a discussion of some of these problems.

12. Agee's comments about the success of Jean Simmon's performance in *Hamlet* exemplify this. *Agee on Film*, I, 392—93.

Chapter Six

1. *Agee on Film*, I, 223.

2. *Ibid.*, p. 224.

3. "Intermission in the Lobby," in *Let Us Now Praise Famous Men*, p. 357.

4. Interview with Father James H. Flye, New York City, August 25, 1969. See also Mayo, p. 201.

5. See, for instance, Perry, p. 139.

6. Agee's comments in his voice letter to Father Flye confirm this (Caedmon TC 2042).

7. Quoted in Davis, "Two Deaths in the Family," p. 11.

8. *Ibid.*, p. 20.

9. Interview with Father Flye, August 25, 1969.

10. "The Nation," *Time*, XLVI (August 20, 1945), 20.

11. *Letters*, p. 153.

12. "Monsieur Verdoux," Autograph manuscript draft with autograph revisions, [1947 May—June], University of Texas Library.

13. "Popular Religion," Typed carbon copy, n.d., University of Texas Library.

14. [Christmas 1945] Autograph working draft with autograph emendations, n.d., University of Texas Library.

15. *Collected Poems*, p. 161.

16. *The Collected Short Prose of James Agee*. The essay originally appeared in *Politics* (April, 1946). All subsequent references are noted parenthetically.

17. This poem is a variant for one which Fitzgerald includes in *The Collected Poems*. "November 1945," Typed carbon copy with autograph emendations, n.d., University of Texas Library.

18. These sonnets originally appeared as part of my "Agee in the Forties" [Unpublished Poetry and fiction by Agee] in the *Texas Quarterly*, XI (Spring, 1968), 18—19.

19. "Marx, I agree . . ." Typed manuscript, n.d., University of Texas Library.

20. *Collected Poems*, 68—69; 163.

21. Catalogued with "If, in the darkness where still a little while," Autograph manuscript with emendations, n.d., University of Texas Library.

22. [Unidentified story; outline and notes] Autograph manuscript with

autograph emendations, n.d., University of Texas Library.

23. *Collected Short Prose*, pp. 143—44.

24. [Unidentified story: "All through the night . . ."] Autograph manuscript with autograph revisions [9 pp.] n.d. The poems are catalogued with [Unidentified play]: Autograph manuscript, working draft, incomplete with autograph emendations [7 pp.] n.d., University of Texas Library.

Chapter Seven

1. "For several years I reviewed movies . . ." See note 5 for preface.

2. [Unidentified television or screenplay] Autograph manuscript working draft with autograph revisions [62 pp.] [c. 1948], University of Texas Library.

3. The article was originally published in *Partisan Review*, and is reprinted in *Agee on Film*, I, 404—10.

4. *Agee on Flim*, I, 275.

5. *Letters*, pp. 194—95.

6. See Barson's clear discussion in *A Way of Seeing*, p. 168.

7. *Ibid.*, p. 169.

8. "The Film Writer," *Commonweal*, LXXII (April 29, 1960), 135.

9. Perry, *op. cit.*, p. 147.

10. Ohlin, *op. cit.*, p. 150.

11. William S. Pechter, "On Agee on Film," *Sight and Sound* XXXIII (Summer, 1964), 148—53.

12. *Agee on Film*, Five Film Scripts (New York: 1967), II, 362—63.

13. Barson, *A Way of Seeing*, p. 173.

14. Seib, *op. cit.*, p. 110.

15. "A Memoir," p. 56.

16. Typed carbon copy letter to David Bradley, Saturday, 26 June, 1953, University of Texas Library.

17. Pechter, *op. cit.*, p. 153.

18. "Noa Noa" Autograph manuscript working draft incomplete with autograph revision [120 pp.] [1953], University of Texas Library.

19. "Noa Noa" Autograph working draft incomplete with autograph revisions [120 pp.] [1953], University of Texas Library.

20. Mayer Levin, "Abraham Lincoln Through the Picture Tube," *Reporter*, 8 (April 14, 1953), p. 31.

21. "Mr. Lincoln," Synopsis and miscellaneous autograph manuscripts with emendations [67 pp.], University of Texas Library.

22. [A Tanglewood Story] Typed carbon copy manuscript [225 pp.] accompanied by autograph working draft, University of Texas Library.

23. Barson, *A Way of Seeing*, p. 182.

24. Dwight Macdonald, *Against the American Grain*, (New York, 1962), p. 164.

Chapter Eight

1. The 1943 date is an approximate one assigned by Macdonald.

2. *Letters*, p. 152.

3. That the use of the atomic bomb was disturbing to Agee is discussed by Barson, *A Way of Seeing*, p. 129 ff.

4. Catalogued as (1) Outline and notes for an adaptation of William Shakespeare's *Macbeth* [10 pp.]; (2) "He shall kill his father: marry his mother" [play] Autograph working draft fragment [11 pp.], University of Texas Library.

5. Caedman TC 2042.

6. "A Mother's Tale," *Collected Short Prose*, pp. 221—43. Subsequent references are noted parenthetically.

7. "1928 Story," *The Texas Quarterly*, XI (Spring, 1968), 23—37. Subsequent references are noted parenthetically.

8. *Letters*, p. 152.

9. Seib, *op. cit.*, argues that the novella contains "some of Agee's most complex symbolism" pp. 69—73.

10. Ohlin demonstrates how the emphasis within the chapel is static (p. 186).

11. *The Morning Watch* (Boston, 1951), p. 119. Subsequent references are noted parenthetically.

12. The morning watch: pages of incomplete drafts (on sheet headed "Notes") n.d., University of Texas Library.

13. *Ibid.*

14. Richard Chase, "Sense and Sensibility," *Kenyon Review*, XIII (Autumn, 1951), 691.

15. The morning watch: pages of incomplete drafts, *op. cit.*

16. F. W. Dupee, "Pride of Maturity," *The Nation*, CLXXII (April 28, 1951), 401.

17. The morning watch: pages of incomplete drafts, *op. cit.*

18. The morning watch: Note, typed and typed carbon copy with autograph emendation, (3 pp.) n.d., University of Texas Library.

19. See Ohlin, p. 190; and John S. Phillipson, "Character, Theme, and Symbol in *The Morning Watch*," *Western Humanities Review*, XV (Autumn, 1961), p. 367 for development of this ironic point.

20. Working notes, *op. cit.*

21. Working notes, autograph manuscript, the morning watch, University of Texas Library.

22. Ohlin, *op. cit.*, p. 188.

23. Mayo, *op. cit.*, documents Agee's approval of a review by Robert Phelps which suggests the story deals with "the abrasively self-conscious sensibility usually identified with an artist as a young man." ("Texture of Life," *Freeman*, I [August 27, 1951] 767.) p. 234.

24. *Letters*, p. 184.

25. *Ibid.*, p. 175.

26. "Religion and the Intellectuals," *Partisan Review*, XVII (February, 1950), 112.

27. *Letters*, p. 181.

Chapter Nine

1. [A death in the family] Autograph manuscripts, with "Notes 1909—1916," 20 pp. n.d., University of Texas Library.

2. See my "The Manuscript and the Text of James Agee's *A Death in the Family*," *Papers of the Bibliographical Society of America*, LXV (Third Quarter, 1971), 257—66.

3. See J. Douglas Perry, Jr. "Thematic Counterpoint in *A Death in The Family*: The Function of the Six Extra Scenes," *Novel*, V (Spring, 1972), 234-41; also my "*A Death in the Family* and Agee's Projections," in volume III of *Proof*.

4. [A death in the family: Notes and fragments] Autograph manuscript (6 pp.), n.d., University of Texas Library.

5. *Ibid.*

6. Compare Seib's assumption that the italicized parts "are seemingly not essential to the main narrative," p. 79.

7. Leslie Fiedler, "Encounter with Death," *New Republic*, CXXXVII (December 9, 1957), 25.

8. Alfred Kazin, *Contemporaries*, (Boston, 1962), p. 187.

9. Ihab Hassan, *Radical Innocence: Studies in the Contemporary American Novel* (New York, 1961), p. 105.

10. A letter of Agee's in admiration of Malcom Lowry's fiction suggests some of what he accomplished in *A Death*. Typed carbon copy letter to Albert Erskine, February 3, 1947, University of Texas Library.

11. See Perry, p. 241.

12. *A Death in the Family* (New York, 1967). All subsequent references are noted parenthetically.

13. Robert Phelps, "The Genius of James Agee," *National Review*, IV (December 7, 1957), 524.

14. In notes "1909—1916" and autograph miscellaneous pages Agee wrote about what he and his sister did on days surrounding the funeral "doing and being archetypal things and unaware of it."

15. See Ohlin, p. 202, where he connects Agee's detailed method with Agee's concept from film criticism about "excesses of energy."

16. Richard H. Rupp, *Celebration in Postwar American Fiction* (Coral Gables, 1970), p. 110.

17. Macdonald, *Against the American Grain*, p. 147.

18. Interview with Father James H. Flye, New York City, August 25, 1969. See also Mayo, pp. 34—35.

19. "Dream Sequence" is printed in my "Agee in the Forties," *Texas Quarterly*, XI (Spring, 1968), 38—46. All subsequent references are noted parenthetically.

20. Compare the anonymous *Time* magazine review, LVII (April 23, 1951), 119, or Barson's comments in *A Way of Seeing* about "Knoxville: Summer of 1915," pp. 68—69.

21. Because the passage differs so in tone, it has even been argued that it may have served as an appendix for the book, Concannon, p. 126.

22. Barson, *A Way of Seeing*, p. 150.

23. Ohlin, *Agee.*, p. 197.

Chapter Ten

1. "A Memoir," p. 55.

2. Interview with Allen Tate, Sewanee, Tennessee, April 3, 1971.

3. Remarks made by Robert Fitzgerald at memorial dinner for Agee, St. Andrew's School, St. Andrews, Tennessee, October 14, 1972.

4. See note 29 of chapter 4.

5. Draft Lyrics for Candide. Catalogued as [Unidentified ·play: fragments] 8 pp., University of Texas Library.

6. "The absolute fundamental: it is democratic." Autograph manuscript with autograph emendations [5 pp. on 4 leaves] n.d., University of Texas Library.

7. Interview with Father James H. Flye, New York City, August 25, 1969.

Selected Bibliography

PRIMARY SOURCES

Books

Permit Me Voyage. New Haven: Yale University Press, 1934.
Let Us Now Praise Famous Men. Boston: Houghton Mifflin, 1941.
The Morning Watch. Boston: Houghton Mifflin, 1951.
A Death in the Family. New York: McDowell, Obolensky, 1957.
Agee on Film: Reviews and Comments. New York: McDowell, Obolensky, 1958.
Agee on Film, Vol II: *Five Film Scripts*. New York: McDowell, Obolensky, 1960.
Let Us Now Praise Famous Men. 2d ed., includes foreword by Walker Evans. Boston: Houghton Mifflin, 1960.
The Letters of James Agee to Father Flye. Edited by James H. Flye. New York: George Brazilier, 1962.
Four Early Stories by James Agee. Collected by Elena Harap. West Branch, Iowa: The Cummington Press, 1964.
The Collected Short Prose of James Agee. Edited, and with "A Memoir" by Robert Fitzgerald. Boston: Houghton Mifflin, 1968.
The Collected Poems of James Agee. Edited, and with introduction, by Robert Fitzgerald. Boston: Houghton Mifflin, 1968.
A Way of Seeing. (Introduction for a book of photographs by Helen Levitt.) New York: Viking, 1965.
The Letters of James Agee to Father Flye. 2d ed., includes letters of Flye to Agee. Boston: Houghton Mifflin, 1971.

Edited Manuscript Material

"Agee in the Forties, Unpublished Poetry and Fiction by James Agee"
(includes "1928 Story," "Dream Sequence," and a variant chapter for
A Death in the Family). Edited, and with introduction. ("Agee in the
Forties: The Struggle to be a Writer"), by Victor A. Kramer. *The Texas Quarterly*, XI (1968), 9—55.

"Work." The complete chapter as written for *Let Us Now Praise Famous
Men*. Edited, and with introduction. ("The Complete 'Work' Chapter
for James Agee's *Let Us Now Praise Famous Men*"), by Victor A.
Kramer. *The Texas Quarterly*, XV (1972), 27—48.

Manuscripts, Tapes, and Related Material

The James Agee Papers at The Humanities Research Center of the University of Texas at Austin are the most extensive collection of Agee
material. My article in *The Library Chronicle*, VIII (1966) 33—36,
describes those holdings.

Additional collections of Agee material exist at Phillips Exeter Academy
and St. Andrew's School. The Exeter collection includes prints of many
of Agee's films and tapes by or about him. The most notable items in
the St. Andrew's collection are video-tapes made during the week
preceding, and on, October 14, 1972, when the library at St. Andrew's
was dedicated in memory of Agee. Many persons who knew Agee
provided commentary during that occasion.

An additional source is available. "James Agee: A Portrait" is a two-record
set of recordings by Agee and by Father Flye reminiscing about him:
Caedmon TC 2042.

SECONDARY SOURCES

Bibliographies

FABRE, GENEVIEVE. "A Bibliography of the Works of James Agee."
Bulletin of Bibliography, XXIV (May—August, 1965) 145—48, 163—66.

"Bibliography." In *The Harvard Advocate Commemorative to James Agee*.
LV (February, 1972), 49—53. Includes brief listing of critical books and
articles on Agee.

Books, Articles, Commentaries, and Reviews

BARSON, ALFRED T. *A Way of Seeing, A Critical Study of James Agee*.
Amherst: University of Massachusetts Press, 1972. Careful study of the
development of Agee's artistic consciousness.

BROUGHTON, GEORGE and PANTHEA R. "Agee and Autonomy."
Southern Humanities Review, IV (1970), 101—11. Account of Agee's
writing with special attention to the concept of individualism.

CHASE, RICHARD. "Sense and Sensibility." *Kenyon Review,* XIII (Autumn, 1951), 688—91. Perceptive early review of *The Morning Watch;* emphasizes its problems of symbolism.

CHESNICK, EUGENE. "The Plot Against Fiction." *The Southern Literary Journal,* IV (1972), 48—67. Attempt to demonstrate that Agee's technique precludes the use of the imagination.

FIEDLER, LESLIE. "Encounter with Death," *New Republic,* CXXXVII (December 9, 1957), 25—26. Clear account of the novel's function.

FROHOCK, W. M. "James Agee: The Question of Wasted Talent." In *The Novel of Violence in America.* Dallas: Southern Methodist University Press, 1957. Overview of Agee's life and work; example of critical disappointment with his literary production.

HOLDER, ALAN. "Encounter in Alabama: Agee and the Tenant Farmer." *Virginia Quarterly Review,* XLII (Spring, 1966), 189—206. Analysis of how *Famous Men* necessitated both movement toward and away from the particularity observed.

HYNES, SAMUEL. "James Agee: *Let Us Now Praise Famous Men.*" In *Landmarks in American Writings,* ed. Hennig Cohen. New York: Basic Books, 1969. Overview of the method developed by Agee to reveal human actuality.

KRAMER, VICTOR A. "The Manuscript and the text of James Agee's *A Death in the Family.*" *The Papers of the Bibliographical Society of America,* LXV (Third Quarter, 1971), 257—66. Results of a collation of the pencil manuscript and text which reveal the difficulties editors faced and some of the errors which resulted.

———. "James Agee's Unpublished Manuscript and His Emphasis on Religious Emotion in *The Morning Watch.*" *Tennessee Studies in Literature,* XVIII (1972), 159—64. Explanation of manuscript notes and alternate manuscript to clarify Agee's intention.

———. "Agee and Plans for the Criticism of Popular Culture." *The Journal of Popular Culture,* V (1972), 755—66. Account of Agee's projections about criticism of popular culture based largely on unpublished manuscript materials.

———. "Agee's *Let Us Now Praise Famous Men:* Image of Tenant Life." *The Mississippi Quarterly,* XXV (1972), 405—17. Critical analysis; demonstrates that, while Agee's presence is crucial to the book, the text provides a clear image of a way of life.

———. "Agee's Use of Regional Material in *A Death in the Family.*" *Appalachian Journal,* I (Autumn, 1972), 72—80. Analysis of Agee's reliance upon Tennessee material along with an edited variant excluded from the composite text.

———. "Agee and His Projections." *Proof,* vol III (1973). Description and analysis of the alternate, variant, and note manuscript which accompanied the composite manuscript for *A Death in the Family*.

LARSEN, ERLING. *James Agee*. Minneapolis: University of Minnesota Press, 1971. Brief overview of Agee's life and works; helpful introductory remarks about the major works.

MACDONALD, DWIGHT. "James Agee." In *Against the American Grain*. New York: Random House, 1965. Memoir and survey of Agee's writing; provides a succinct introduction.

MADDEN, DAVID ed., *Remembering James Agee*. Baton Rouge; Louisiana State University Press, 1974. Essays, recollections, and remembrances by various persons who knew Agee, including his widow, Mia. Includes an introduction by the editor.

OHLIN, PETER H. *Agee*. New York: Obolensky, 1966. Critical analysis of all important writing by Agee available preceding 1966; detailed commentary about each of Agee's books including the criticism and screenplays.

OULAHAN, RICHARD. "A Cult Grew Around a Many-Sided Writer." *Life*, LV (November 1, 1963), 69—72. Popular account of the personality and writings of Agee.

PERRY, J. DOUGLAS, JR. "Thematic Counterpoint in *A Death in the Family*: The Function of the Six Extra Scenes." *Novel*, V (Spring, 1972), 234—41. Explanation of the nonsequential parts of the published novel.

PHILLIPSON, JOHN S. "Character, Theme, and Symbol in *The Morning Watch*." *Western Humanities Review*, XV (Autumn, 1961), 359—67. Critical analysis demonstrates the intricate structure of the novella.

RAMSEY, ROGER. "The Double Structure of *The Morning Watch*." *Studies in the Novel*, IV (Fall, 1972), 494—03. An argument that the narrative and the "triptych" structure balance and support each other.

RUOFF, GENE W. "A Death in the Family: Agee's 'Unfinished' Novel." In *The Fifties*, ed. by Warren French. Deland, Fla: Everett/Edwards, 1970. Introductory essay about the predominant ideas within the novel.

RUPP, RICHARD H. "James Agee: The Elegies of Innocence." In *Celebration in Post-War American Fiction*. Coral Gables: University of Miami, 1972. Perceptive essay about the main themes in *The Morning Watch* and *A Death in the Family*, where Agee laments the passing of innocence.

SEIB, KENNETH. *James Agee: Promise and Fulfillment*. Pittsburgh: University of Pittsburgh Press, 1968. Brief overview of Agee's literary career and important writings; but often poorly documented and sometimes incorrect.

STANFORD, DONALD E. "The Poetry of James Agee: The Art of

Recovery." *The Southern Review*, X (Spring, 1974), xvi—xix. Call for the recognition of Agee who successfully assimilated earlier styles into his modern poems.

STOTT, WILLIAM. *Documentary Expression and Thirties America*. New York: Oxford University Press, 1973. Useful study of the documentary genre as it developed in the 1930s with separate chapters on Evans's photographs and Agee's text of *Let Us Now Praise Famous Men*.

TOWNSEND, R. C. "The Possibilities of Field Work." *College English*, XXXIV (January, 1973), 481—99. Description of many works, including *Let Us Now Praise Famous Men*, and their use in English courses to relate literature to living.

WENSBERG, ERIK. "Celebration, Adoration and Wonder." *Nation*, CXCI (November 26, 1960), 417—18. One of the most perceptive early accounts of the value of *Let Us Now Praise Famous Men*.

Index

(The works of Agee are listed following his name.)